The Complete Leadership Operating System

Lucas Customer Satisfaction Model 10

LCSM10

Faith Edition

For Organizational Alignment
Sustainable Growth
Customer Satisfaction

Dr. Nathanael J. Lucas
Management Action Group LLC

Published by: Nathanael J. Lucas

Printed in the United States of America
ISBN: 979-8-9945041-1-6

A Note from the Author

This work was originally developed as a doctoral dissertation, then later developed as a tool to ensure clarity, cohesion, and practical application. It reflects the perspective of a practitioner, business owner, and consultant committed to building durable leadership architecture.

The focus of this book is structural integrity. Its purpose is to provide leaders with disciplined tools for alignment, governance, and long-term organizational strength.

Thank you for engaging these ideas thoughtfully and applying them with conviction.

If you would like to learn more about my work or how I support small organizations, please visit:
www.managementactiongroup.com

I would be honored to connect with you.

Contents

How to Use This Book

This work has been written as a leadership operating system. It is designed to govern how organizations think, decide, build, and lead. It is not a curriculum, a devotional, or a motivational resource. It is a strategic leadership framework grounded in biblical conviction, academic research, and operational discipline.

The purpose of this book is to establish the leadership architecture of the Lucas Customer Satisfaction Model 10 (LCSM10). It provides the governing principles, strategic logic, and alignment framework that shape how values, vision, mission, culture, strategy, and policy function as a unified system. Leaders who complete this work will possess the intellectual, theological, and operational foundation required to build aligned organizational structures.

This book prepares leaders for disciplined execution through the LCSM10 Implementation Series. These implementation manuals provide the structured tools, diagnostics, construction models, and alignment instruments necessary to build organizational statements, governance systems, and leadership frameworks with precision and accountability. Leaders should not attempt to construct organizational statements, governance models, or alignment systems without first completing the leadership foundation presented in this book. The effectiveness of the implementation process depends upon a clear understanding of the governing architecture. Alignment cannot be built without first understanding how alignment functions.

This work is intended for senior leadership, boards, executive teams, and founders. It establishes the authority structure of leadership and the stewardship responsibility entrusted to those who govern people, resources, and mission. The implementation manuals then translate this architecture into measurable, repeatable, and enforceable systems.

Together, this book and the LCSM10 Implementation Series form a complete leadership operating system. This book governs. The implementation manuals execute. Leadership stewards both.

After completing this work, and with an understanding of the framework, the next step is disciplined statement construction through the LCSM10 statement workbooks available through managementactiongroup.com.

PART I

FOUNDATIONS OF ORGANIZATIONAL ALIGNMENT

Theological Foundation of the LCSM10 Framework ⟶

The Lucas Customer Satisfaction Model 10 (LCSM10) is built on the conviction that all leadership, authority, and stewardship ultimately belong to God. Scripture establishes that leadership is not self-derived, power is not self-owned, and influence is not self-directed. Leaders do not govern by personal right, professional status, or institutional position. They govern by stewardship under divine authority.

This framework submits first to biblical truth, then applies academic research and organizational discipline as instruments of faithful leadership. Scripture is not an inspirational supplement to this model. It is the highest governing authority.

"All authority is given unto me in heaven and in earth." Matthew 28:18 (KJV)

Leadership is therefore not ownership. It is accountability.

"Moreover it is required in stewards, that a man be found faithful." 1 Corinthians 4:2 (KJV)

The purpose of the LCSM10 is not merely organizational effectiveness, customer satisfaction, or operational excellence. Its purpose is faithful stewardship of people, resources, mission, and influence entrusted by God. Research informs the model. Structure strengthens the model. Discipline sustains the model. Scripture governs the model.

For churches, ministries, faith-based organizations, and Christian-led enterprises, leadership is not neutral. It is moral. It is spiritual. It is accountable. Every value enforced, every vision pursued, every mission executed, every culture formed, every strategy deployed, and every policy written must stand under the authority of God's Word.

"The fear of the Lord is the beginning of wisdom." Proverbs 9:10 (KJV)

The LCSM10 framework exists to serve that wisdom.

This is a leadership operating system built for those who understand that alignment is not merely organizational. It is theological. It is ethical. It is eternal. Every healthy organization, whether a church, nonprofit, or business, is built on a foundation of shared convictions, clear direction, disciplined execution, and principled governance. When these elements are misaligned, even the most passionate teams struggle. Vision becomes fragmented. Strategy becomes reactive. Culture becomes inconsistent. Policies become either ignored or overbearing. Over time, trust erodes, morale weakens, and organizational drift sets in.

LCSM10 was developed to address a persistent leadership problem. Most organizations operate with good intentions but without coherent alignment. Values exist without enforcement. Vision exists without execution. Mission exists without ownership. Culture forms without design. Strategy moves without restraint. Policy exists without purpose. The result is fragmentation.

Here, leaders will examine the costs of organizational misalignment, engage with the research foundation of customer-focused leadership, and gain a clear understanding of the LCSM10 leadership architecture. This is not theory for theory's sake. It is a leadership system designed for real organizations, real people, and absolute pressure. It is the infrastructure of trust. It is the engine of sustainability. It is the responsibility of leadership.

The chapters that follow establish the governing framework upon which values, vision, mission, culture, strategy, and policy are built into a single integrated leadership system. These foundations prepare leaders for structured implementation through the LCSM10 application guides and leadership tools that accompany this work. This is where alignment begins.

Chapter 1: Building Customer-Focused Clarity and Direction

This chapter establishes the foundation for the LCSM10 by clarifying how customer-focused purpose and direction are formed, sustained, and protected over time. It introduces leadership conditions that allow values, mission, and vision to function as operational instruments rather than aspirational language. The focus is not on organizational failure, but on how clarity is built, maintained, and reinforced as organizations grow and complexity increases. This chapter prepares the reader to understand why disciplined construction of organizational statements is necessary for sustaining trust, consistency, and customer satisfaction.

Why Organizations Lose Clarity, Direction, and Customer Trust →

Organizations rarely fail because they lack passion, intelligence, or effort. They fail because they lose clarity about whom they serve and where they are going. This loss of direction is gradual and often invisible to those living inside it, yet its effects are felt most clearly by customers.

The erosion begins when values are stated but not enforced, when the mission is communicated but not practiced, and when the vision is discussed without being translated into consistent action. Culture becomes reactive rather than intentional. Strategy responds to pressure rather than to purpose. Policies exist on paper but fail to protect what matters. Over time, organizations become internally busy while externally inconsistent. Customers experience mixed signals, uneven service, and unmet expectations. Trust weakens, not because intent is absent, but because direction is unclear and inconsistently lived.

The Lucas Customer Satisfaction Model 10 (LCSM10) was developed to address this problem directly. It exists because customer trust and satisfaction are not sustained by inspiration alone, but by clarity of purpose and direction consistently expressed through organizational behavior. Doctoral research conducted by Lucas (2018) examined whether customer-focused organizational statements are associated with customer satisfaction outcomes. Statistical testing revealed a significant positive relationship between the customer focus scores of mission statements and customer satisfaction scores, $r_s(82) = .390$, $p < .01$, and a significant positive relationship between the customer focus scores of vision statements and customer satisfaction scores, $r_s(82) = .344$, $p < .05$. This research forms the foundation of the LCSM10 framework (Lucas, N. J., 2018, Identifying relationships between the customer focus scores of mission and vision statements and customer satisfaction scores, Doctoral dissertation, Grand Canyon University).

Within the LCSM10 framework, these findings rest on the prior construction of a clearly defined Values Statement, which establishes the governing beliefs and decision boundaries that inform both mission and vision. Values shape how purpose and direction are interpreted, protected, and prioritized. When values are clear and consistently applied, mission and vision function as operational guides rather than aspirational language. In this way, Values, Vision, and Mission serve as measurable leadership tools that influence decision-making consistency, organizational behavior, and customer experience.

Within the LCSM10, Values serve as the foundational authority from which organizational culture, strategy, and policy are formed, all of which operate in support of and alignment with the organization's Mission and Vision. Alignment is not the goal; it is the condition that allows customer-focused purpose and direction to be lived consistently.

This chapter establishes the leadership problem the LCSM10 is designed to solve. It examines how organizations lose directional clarity, why good intentions are insufficient to sustain customer trust, and how inconsistency between purpose and practice undermines satisfaction, credibility, and long-term viability. The central leadership responsibility is clear: customer-focused direction must be intentionally defined and consistently reinforced. When it is not, misalignment follows, and customer trust erodes.

The patterns described in this chapter are not isolated failures; they follow a predictable structure. Understanding that structure requires a clear framework that explains how purpose, direction, and leadership systems are meant to function together.

Foundational Logic of The *LCSM10* Framework

Organizational effectiveness follows a clear and intentional progression. Values define priorities, establishing what the organization believes and what it will consistently protect. Vision defines customer-focused direction, articulating where the organization is going in service of that purpose. Mission defines customer-focused purpose, clarifying why the organization exists and whom it serves. Alignment ensures that purpose and direction are lived consistently, shaping decisions, behavior, and execution across the organization. When these elements function together, the result is not internal coherence alone, but measurable customer satisfaction, which serves as the ultimate outcome and validation of directional clarity.

Defining Customers, Internal Alignment, and Stakeholder Priority

Customer focus within the LCSM10 framework must be clearly defined to prevent confusion, misapplication, and diluted accountability. Organizations often use the terms customers, stakeholders, staff, and participants interchangeably, which leads to inconsistent decision-making and fragmented priorities. Without clear definitions, leadership cannot maintain alignment, and organizational systems begin to serve internal activity rather than external purpose.

Within the LCSM10 framework, a customer is defined as the individual or group who directly receives the outcome of the organization's mission. Customers are the recipients of value creation. They are the individuals whose experience ultimately determines whether the organization is fulfilling its stated purpose. In a business context, this may be the paying client. In a church context, this includes both congregants and those the church is called to reach. In all cases, customers are those served by the mission, not those managing it.

It is also necessary to distinguish between internal and external customers. Internal customers consist of employees, staff, and volunteers who operate within the organization and rely on internal systems, leadership, and communication to perform effectively. External customers consist of those outside the organizational structure who directly receive the organization's services, care, or output. While internal alignment is necessary for operational effectiveness, it is not the ultimate measure of success. Organizations do not exist to serve internal systems; they exist to serve external customers through those systems.

A third category, often emphasized in leadership literature, is the concept of stakeholders. Stakeholders include any individual or group with an interest in the organization's performance, such as donors, board members, partners, regulators, or community influencers. While stakeholders are important and must be considered in governance and decision-making, they do not occupy the same role as customers within the LCSM10 framework.

Within this model, customers take precedence over stakeholders because they are the direct recipients of mission execution and the primary drivers of measurable outcomes.

Stakeholders may influence the organization, but customers validate it. An organization may satisfy stakeholders in the short term through reporting, communication, or compliance, but if it fails to serve its customers effectively, long-term sustainability, trust, and credibility will decline.

Misalignment often occurs when organizations elevate stakeholder preferences or internal comfort above customer-focused purpose. This results in systems that protect internal processes, preserve existing structures, or respond to external pressures while neglecting the actual experience of those being served. Over time, this shift produces inconsistency, weakens trust, and undermines the mission itself.

The LCSM10 framework corrects this misalignment by establishing a clear order of priority. Values govern decision boundaries. Vision defines customer-focused direction. Mission defines customer-focused purpose. Culture, strategy, and policy function to support consistent execution. Customers remain the central reference point for evaluating whether alignment is being achieved. Internal systems support this outcome. Stakeholders inform it, but do not replace it.

Clarity in these distinctions is not theoretical. It is operational. When leadership understands who the customer is, how internal systems support that customer, and how stakeholder influence is properly positioned, decision-making becomes more consistent, alignment strengthens, and customer satisfaction becomes a measurable and sustainable outcome.

Why Organizations Lose Focus Over Time →

Most organizations do not lose focus because they lack vision or passion. They lose focus because clarity is not intentionally maintained. In the beginning, leaders know exactly why the organization exists. The mission is clear. The work feels personal. Decisions are made close to purpose. As the organization grows, however, complexity increases. New staff are hired. New programs are launched. New pressures emerge. Urgent needs begin to compete with important priorities. Over time, four common patterns emerge.

First, success creates distraction. What once required discipline becomes routine. Leaders begin pursuing new opportunities before strengthening core purpose, slowly shifting attention away from what originally mattered most.

Second, growth creates complexity. More people, more systems, and more responsibilities increase the likelihood of miscommunication and inconsistency. Without clear direction, focus becomes harder to sustain across the organization.

Third, pressure encourages reactionary leadership. Instead of leading with intention, leaders begin responding to immediate demands. Strategy narrows into survival, and long-term direction receives less attention.

Fourth, time creates distance from the original mission. New leaders did not experience the founding context. The original vision becomes history rather than a living guide for decisions.

When these forces combine, organizational focus erodes. Decision-making becomes fragmented. Priorities blur. Culture weakens. Trust declines. This loss of focus does not occur suddenly. It develops gradually and often goes unnoticed until the cost becomes visible. For this reason, maintaining focus is not a one-time activity. It is an ongoing leadership discipline that protects the organization's purpose, direction, and the experience of those it serves.

The Cost of Misalignment →

Misalignment is one of the most costly leadership failures an organization can experience. It rarely appears as a single dramatic breakdown. It develops gradually through inconsistent decisions, unclear priorities, an unmanaged culture, and disconnected systems. Over time, what once felt focused and purposeful becomes fragmented and reactive.

When values are not reflected in daily behavior, trust weakens. When vision is not reinforced through strategy, direction becomes blurred. When mission is not protected by policy, decision-making becomes inconsistent. When culture is left unmanaged, standards erode. When strategy is disconnected from beliefs, momentum becomes chaotic. When policy lacks purpose, governance becomes ineffective. Each breakdown compounds the next, creating an organization that appears busy but lacks coherence.

The visible costs surface first. Confusion increases, morale declines, and conflict becomes more frequent. Decision-making slows as priorities become unclear, accountability weakens, and performance grows inconsistent. Leaders find themselves spending more time managing internal friction than advancing the mission the organization exists to serve.

The hidden costs follow more quietly. High performers disengage as confidence erodes, customers begin to lose trust, and reputation weakens over time. Resources are wasted correcting preventable problems, leadership credibility declines, and the organization gradually works harder while producing less, expending energy on issues that strong alignment would have prevented.

Misalignment is not a cultural problem alone. It is not a strategy problem alone. It is not a policy problem alone. Misalignment is a leadership problem, and its cost is paid in trust, momentum, reputation, and long-term sustainability.

When Values Exist Without Enforcement

When values exist without enforcement, they become symbolic rather than operational. Organizations may publicly affirm integrity, accountability, excellence, or service, but without leadership discipline, those values fail to shape daily behavior. Over time, values become slogans on walls rather than standards that govern decisions, relationships, and accountability.

Research consistently shows that organizational statements only influence culture and performance when they are translated into lived behavior. Values define identity and conviction, while leadership behavior determines whether those convictions become operational. Values that are not reinforced through leadership action, evaluation systems, and accountability structures lose authority and credibility. In such environments, culture fills the gap with habit, personality, urgency, or convenience rather than shared standards.

Values are not aspirational ideals. They are governing principles that must shape how people are treated, how problems are resolved, how priorities are set, and how pressure is handled. When values are clear and practiced consistently, organizations experience higher levels of trust, alignment, and customer satisfaction. When values are vague, decorative, or inconsistently applied, satisfaction declines, trust erodes, and long-term sustainability is compromised .

When Vision Exists Without Strategy

When vision exists without strategy, organizations develop ambition without direction. Leaders may articulate compelling future goals, inspiring language, and bold aspirations, yet without a clear execution plan, that vision remains conceptual rather than operational. People know where the organization claims it is going, but they do not know how it intends to get there.

Within the LCSM10, strategy is not a reaction to market pressure or opportunity alone. It is a deliberate expression of organizational values in pursuit of vision and mission. Strategy translates values into prioritized action, determining not only what the organization will pursue but also how it will pursue it. When strategy is detached from values, it becomes opportunistic. When strategy is detached from mission and vision, it loses direction.

Vision without strategy creates frustration. Teams hear calls for growth, impact, and excellence, yet lack priorities, timelines, and resource alignment. Decision-making becomes inconsistent because there is no agreed-upon path forward. Opportunities are pursued reactively rather than intentionally. Energy is scattered across too many initiatives, each competing for attention, funding, and leadership support.

Over time, vision loses credibility. Staff and stakeholders begin to view it as rhetorical rather than direction. Momentum slows because progress is difficult to measure. Leaders become trapped in a constant state of motion without meaningful advancement. The organization remains busy, yet forward movement becomes difficult to verify.

Customer-focused mission and vision statements influence satisfaction only when they are translated into operational clarity and strategic consistency. Vision creates expectation. Strategy creates confidence. When the two are disconnected, trust erodes and organizational alignment weakens (Lucas, 2018).

Within the LCSM10 framework, vision defines destination, while strategy defines disciplined movement shaped by organizational values. Vision answers the question of where the organization is going. Strategy answers how it will get there in a manner consistent with what the organization believes and prioritizes. When vision is present without strategy, organizations dream well but execute poorly. Alignment requires both.

When Mission Exists Without Culture →

Within the LCSM10, culture does not generate values; it reflects them. Culture emerges from the consistent application of values and cannot correct misalignment created by unclear or poorly constructed values. When mission exists without culture, organizations possess purpose without practice. Leaders may clearly articulate why the organization exists and whom it serves, yet when daily behavior does not reflect that mission, the mission remains theoretical rather than lived. People may be able to recite the mission statement, but they do not experience it in how decisions are made, how problems are addressed, or how individuals are treated.

Mission without culture produces inconsistency. The organization claims one identity while operating according to another. Teams are told what matters, yet are rewarded for something different. Customers and congregants hear promises that are not reflected in service, communication, or care. Over time, the mission loses authority because it is not reinforced through shared standards, behavioral expectations, and lived practice.

Culture serves as the delivery system for the mission. It determines whether purpose becomes operational or remains aspirational. When culture is left unmanaged, habit replaces intention, convenience replaces conviction, and urgency replaces discernment. The organization may continue to speak about its mission, but its actions communicate a conflicting message.

The research supports this connection. Mission clarity influences satisfaction only when it is translated into consistent organizational behavior. When the mission is reinforced through aligned leadership practices and coherent cultural norms, trust and satisfaction increase. When the mission is disconnected from culture, satisfaction declines, and organizational credibility weakens (Lucas, 2018).

Within the LCSM10 framework, mission defines purpose, while culture defines practice. Mission answers why the organization exists. Culture answers the question of how that purpose is lived each day. When a mission exists without culture, organizations know who they are intended to be, but fail to become it.

When Policy Exists Without Purpose →

When policy exists without purpose, organizations develop rules without reason. Procedures multiply, approvals slow decision-making, and compliance replaces conviction. Policies become administrative obstacles rather than leadership tools, enforced inconsistently and followed selectively. Over time, people stop viewing policy as protection and begin experiencing it as bureaucracy.

Policy without purpose generates resentment. Staff feel constrained rather than supported. Leaders rely on rules in place of judgment. Accountability becomes mechanical rather than relational. Decision-making loses flexibility because policies are followed out of fear rather than understanding. In these environments, governance becomes rigid where wisdom is required and permissive where firmness is necessary.

Policy exists to protect what matters most. It is designed to guard values, reinforce mission, sustain culture, and safeguard strategy. When policy is disconnected from these foundations, it loses legitimacy. Compliance becomes conditional. People follow rules when oversight is present and ignore them when it is absent. The organization becomes vulnerable to ethical drift, inconsistent discipline, and reputational risk.

The research supports this relationship. Organizational clarity and alignment strengthen trust and satisfaction when leadership systems consistently reinforce stated commitments. Policies that reflect organizational purpose increase accountability and credibility. Policies that exist in isolation weaken engagement and invite inconsistency (Lucas, 2018).

Within the LCSM10 framework, policy is not control; it is stewardship. Policy answers how values are protected, how culture is sustained, and how strategy is preserved under pressure. When policy exists without purpose, organizations enforce rules but fail to lead with integrity.

Learning Outcomes

Organizational misalignment rarely results from a lack of passion or effort. It develops when clarity is not maintained, and leadership systems are not intentionally reinforced. As organizations grow, complexity increases, pressure rises, and distance from the founding mission expands. Over time, focus erodes, decision-making fragments, culture weakens, and trust declines.

We have identified four common leadership breakdowns that create drift: values without enforcement, vision without strategy, mission without culture, and policy without purpose. Each represents a failure to translate belief into behavior and intention into execution. When these elements are disconnected, organizations become busy but ineffective, working harder while producing less.

Misalignment carries visible and hidden costs. Confusion increases, morale declines, conflict rises, and accountability weakens. High performers disengage, customers lose confidence, reputations erode, and leadership credibility suffers. The organization expends energy correcting problems that strong alignment would have prevented. Sustaining customer-focused purpose and direction is not accidental; it is a leadership discipline that protects clarity, reinforces consistency, and ultimately shapes customer trust and satisfaction.

With this foundation in place, the chapters that follow will examine how each leadership component contributes to sustaining customer-focused purpose and direction. Before organizations can construct effective values, mission, and vision statements, they must understand the structural conditions that either support or undermine clarity over time.

Chapter 2: The Research Foundation of LCSM10

Why Organizational Clarity Drives Satisfaction, Trust, and Sustainability

This chapter establishes the intellectual and empirical foundation of the LCSM10 framework. It demonstrates that organizational alignment is not a leadership trend or philosophical preference. It is a measurable, research-supported driver of customer satisfaction, trust, loyalty, and long-term organizational health.

The purpose of this chapter is to anchor the LCSM10 model in scholarship and evidence. It introduces the research underpinning the framework, including Lucas (2018). It explains why customer-focused mission and vision statements influence satisfaction only when they are clear, aligned, and consistently reinforced through leadership systems.

Leaders will see that clarity is not abstract. It is operational. It influences decision-making, behavior, culture, and performance. When leadership language is disciplined and aligned, trust increases. When leadership language is vague or inconsistent, satisfaction declines, and organizational drift accelerates. This chapter establishes that alignment is measurable, leadership clarity is consequential, and organizational health is not accidental. LCSM10 is not built on opinion. It is built on research, observation, and real-world leadership applications.

Summary of Lucas (2018) ⟶

The Lucas (2018) doctoral research examined the relationship between customer-focused mission and vision statements and customer satisfaction. The study tested whether organizational clarity, specifically how clearly leaders define purpose and direction, has a measurable impact on how customers experience an organization.

The findings demonstrated that mission and vision statements are not merely symbolic. When they are clear, customer-focused, and consistently reinforced through leadership behavior and organizational systems, they contribute to higher levels of customer satisfaction, trust, and long-term loyalty. When they are vague, internally focused, or disconnected from daily operations, they lose influence and credibility.

The Research Confirmed Three Core Principles →

First, clarity matters. Customers respond positively to organizations that know who they are, why they exist, and where they are going.

Second, alignment matters. Mission and vision statements only influence satisfaction when they are supported by leadership behavior, culture, strategy, and policy.

Third, leadership language matters. The way leaders define purpose and direction shapes organizational identity, decision-making, and customer experience.

This research is important to the LCSM10 framework because it provides the empirical foundation for the model. LCSM10 was developed to translate these findings into a practical leadership system. The framework operationalizes research into structure, discipline, and governance, ensuring clarity becomes sustainable rather than situational. In short, LCSM10 exists because Lucas (2018) demonstrated that organizational clarity is not a leadership preference. It is a measurable driver of satisfaction, trust, and long-term organizational health.

Why Values Precede Customer-Focused Purpose and Direction

Lucas's (2018) findings demonstrate that clarity in the customer-focused mission and vision is positively related to customer satisfaction. While the research measured the construction and clarity of mission and vision statements, those statements do not exist or operate in isolation. They are interpreted, applied, and sustained through deeper organizational beliefs that govern behavior over time. Within the LCSM10 framework, those governing beliefs are articulated through values.

Values precede mission and vision because they establish the priorities and boundaries that determine how purpose and direction are understood and enacted. Mission defines why an organization exists and whom it serves. Vision defines where the organization is going in service of that purpose. Values determine what the organization will consistently protect, prioritize, and uphold as it pursues that direction. Without clear values, mission, and vision, mission and vision may be articulated accurately but applied inconsistently, resulting in fragmented behavior and an uneven customer experience.

Customer-focused purpose and direction require more than descriptive language. They require interpretive discipline. Values function as the interpretive filter through which leaders and staff translate mission and vision into decisions, behaviors, and responses under pressure. When values are clearly defined and consistently reinforced, they stabilize how mission and vision are lived across situations, personnel changes, and competing demands. When values are vague, implicit, or inconsistently applied, mission and vision clarity erodes, even if the language itself remains unchanged.

The LCSM10 does not suggest that values replace mission or vision, nor does it claim that values alone generate customer satisfaction. Rather, values provide the structural foundation that allows the customer-focused mission and vision to operate consistently over time. In the absence of values discipline, organizations often experience organizational misalignment, not because their stated purpose or direction is unclear, but because there is no shared agreement about which priorities take precedence when trade-offs arise. This inconsistency is felt most clearly by customers, who experience variation in service, communication, and follow-through.

Lucas (2018) demonstrated that mission and vision clarity influence satisfaction when leadership language is reinforced through organizational systems. Values are the first of those systems. They inform culture by shaping behavioral expectations. They inform strategy by defining acceptable paths and unacceptable shortcuts. They inform policy by clarifying what must be protected regardless of convenience or pressure. In this way, values do not compete with mission and vision; they protect them.

Within the LCSM10 framework, values serve as the governing authority that anchors customer-focused purpose and direction. They ensure that mission and vision remain operational rather than aspirational, stable rather than situational. By preceding mission and vision, values provide the consistency required for leadership clarity to translate into customer trust, satisfaction, and long-term organizational health.

What the Research Did Not Claim

Lucas's (2018) findings establish a significant relationship between customer-focused mission and vision clarity and customer satisfaction. However, the research did not claim that organizational statements function as independent or automatic drivers of satisfaction. Mission and vision language alone do not guarantee trust, loyalty, or consistent customer experience.

The study did not suggest that simply rewriting mission or vision statements produces improved outcomes. Nor did it imply that leadership language substitutes for leadership behavior, culture, strategy, or governance. Customer satisfaction is not the result of isolated wording, but of how purpose and direction are consistently expressed through decisions, actions, and systems over time.

Lucas (2018) also did not claim that customer satisfaction can be sustained without leadership discipline. The relationships identified in the research depend on reinforcement through organizational structures and practices. When mission and vision are articulated clearly but not supported by consistent leadership behavior, their influence diminishes. In such cases, customers experience inconsistency between stated commitments and actual performance.

The LCSM10 framework builds on these findings by addressing what the research intentionally did not prescribe. It does not reinterpret the results, nor does it extend the claims beyond their empirical limits. Instead, it provides a structured leadership framework that translates research-supported clarity into sustained practice. LCSM10 explains how values, culture, strategy, and policy work together to sustain a customer-focused purpose and direction amid growth, pressure, and complexity.

Customer-Focused Mission And Vision

A customer-focused mission and vision place the people an organization serves at the center of its purpose and direction. They define why the organization exists and where it is going in a way that is meaningful not only to internal leadership but also to customers, congregants, and stakeholders. These statements move beyond internal ambition and describe a commitment to real people, real needs, and real impact.

Mission answers the question of purpose. It clarifies who the organization serves, what it provides, and why its work matters. Vision answers the question of direction. It defines the future the organization is pursuing and the outcome it is working to achieve for those it serves. When both are customer-focused, they create a shared understanding of identity and direction that guides decisions, priorities, and behavior.

Lucas (2018) demonstrated that customer-focused mission and vision statements influence satisfaction only when they are clear, intentional, and consistently reinforced through leadership systems. Organizations that articulate purpose and direction in a way that reflects customer needs and expectations build stronger trust and long-term loyalty. Organizations that focus mission and vision inward, toward internal goals or abstract ideals, struggle to translate those statements into meaningful customer experience.

Within the LCSM10 framework, customer-focused mission and vision are not marketing tools. They are leadership instruments. They shape organizational identity, inform strategy, guide culture, and anchor policy. When mission and vision are written with the customer in mind and lived out through disciplined leadership, they become a foundation for sustainable growth, trust, and organizational health.

Statement Clarity And Satisfaction

Statement clarity is one of the most overlooked drivers of organizational health and customer satisfaction. Mission and vision statements shape how an organization understands itself and how it presents itself to the people it serves. When those statements are clear, focused, and meaningful, they provide direction for leadership, alignment for staff, and confidence for customers. When they are vague, generic, or internally focused, they create confusion and weaken trust.

Clarity is not about eloquence. It is about understanding. A clear statement communicates purpose and direction in a way that is easy to grasp, remember, and apply. Leaders know what matters. Staff know what is expected. Customers know what the organization stands for. This shared understanding creates consistency in decision-making, service delivery, and communication.

Lucas (2018) demonstrated that organizations with clear, customer-focused mission and vision statements experience higher levels of customer satisfaction. Clarity strengthens trust because customers can see alignment between what an organization says and what it does. When leadership language is disciplined and consistent, it creates confidence. When leadership language is ambiguous or disconnected from operations, satisfaction declines.

Within the LCSM10 framework, statement clarity is not a branding exercise. It is a leadership responsibility. Clear mission and vision statements become operational tools that guide culture, strategy, and policy. When clarity is maintained, satisfaction grows. When clarity is neglected, drift begins.

From Leadership Clarity to Customer Experience →

From leadership clarity to customer experience, the pathway is behavioral consistency. Customers do not experience mission and vision statements directly; they experience how decisions are made, how problems are handled, and how commitments are honored. When leadership language is clear and customer-focused, it creates predictable patterns of behavior that customers can recognize and trust.

Clarity influences experience through repetition. Consistent priorities shape consistent decisions. Consistent decisions shape consistent service. Over time, customers come to expect a certain level of care, responsiveness, and integrity because leadership purpose and direction are reinforced through daily action. Satisfaction increases not because customers have read the organization's statements, but because they encounter the same values and commitments regardless of whom they interact with or when the interaction occurs.

Lucas (2018) demonstrated that clarity in customer-focused mission and vision is associated with higher satisfaction because it reduces variability. When purpose and direction are well defined and reinforced, organizations respond to customers with greater coherence. When clarity is weak, customer experience becomes dependent on individual discretion rather than shared direction, resulting in inconsistency and diminished trust.

Within the LCSM10 framework, customer experience is the external validation of internal clarity. Mission and vision define intent. Values stabilize interpretation. Culture, strategy, and policy reinforce behavior. When these elements function together, customers experience reliability rather than randomness. Satisfaction grows when expectations are met consistently, not occasionally.

Why Clarity Degrades Without Structural Reinforcement

Clarity is not self-sustaining. Even when mission and vision are well constructed and clearly communicated, their influence diminishes over time if they are not intentionally reinforced. Growth, turnover, pressure, and changing circumstances gradually introduce interpretation gaps that weaken consistency. Without structural reinforcement, clarity becomes situational rather than durable.

Leadership transitions accelerate this erosion. New leaders inherit language without shared context. Decisions are made without reference to original intent. Over time, purpose and direction remain visible in documents but fade in practice. Customers experience this shift as inconsistency, unpredictability, or reduced confidence, even when the organization believes it remains clear.

Lucas (2018) demonstrated that customer satisfaction is associated with clarity that is consistently reinforced. The research implies durability, not momentary precision. When leadership language is supported by systems that repeat, protect, and prioritize customer-focused purpose and direction, satisfaction is sustained. When reinforcement weakens, clarity fragments, and customer experience becomes uneven.

Within the LCSM10 framework, sustaining clarity requires intentional leadership systems. Values anchor interpretation. Culture reinforces behavior. Strategy directs action. Policy protects priorities under pressure. Together, these elements preserve clarity as organizations grow and change. Without this reinforcement, clarity becomes vulnerable to drift, and customer trust becomes difficult to maintain.

Trust, Loyalty, And Long-Term Health

Trust is the currency of every healthy organization. It is built when leadership language, leadership behavior, and customer experience remain aligned over time. Customers and stakeholders develop confidence when they see consistency between what an organization claims to stand for and how it actually operates. When purpose and direction are clear, and when those commitments are reinforced through culture, strategy, and policy, trust becomes durable.

Loyalty follows trust. Customers return when expectations are met consistently. Staff remain committed when leadership is credible. Partners invest when governance is stable. Over time, these relationships create organizational resilience. Growth becomes sustainable rather than reactive. Reputation becomes an asset rather than a risk. Performance becomes predictable rather than volatile.

Lucas (2018) demonstrated that clarity in the customer-focused mission and vision directly contributes to customer satisfaction and long-term loyalty. Organizations that communicate purpose and direction clearly and reinforce commitments through leadership systems build stronger trust and more durable stakeholder relationships. When leadership language is vague or disconnected from daily operations, satisfaction declines, and loyalty weakens.

Within the LCSM10 framework, trust is not a byproduct. It is an outcome of alignment. Loyalty is not accidental. It is earned through consistency. Long-term organizational health is not the result of short-term success. It is built through disciplined leadership, clear purpose, and sustained alignment over time.

Why Leadership Language Matters

Leadership language shapes organizational reality. The words leaders use to define purpose, direction, values, and priorities influence how people think, decide, and act. Mission statements, vision statements, values declarations, strategic priorities, and policies are not neutral. They form the organization's operating narrative.

Language creates expectations. It signals what matters. It frames success. It defines accountability. When leadership language is clear, disciplined, and consistent, it produces shared understanding. Staff know what the organization stands for. Customers know what to expect. Decision-making becomes more consistent because priorities are well defined.

Vague or inconsistent leadership language creates confusion, leading teams to interpret the purpose differently. Leaders send mixed signals. Standards drift. Culture becomes personality-driven rather than principle-driven. Over time, credibility weakens because what is said no longer matches what is experienced.

Lucas (2018) demonstrated that customer-focused mission and vision statements influence satisfaction only when they are clear and reinforced through leadership behavior and organizational systems. Leadership language establishes identity and direction, but its influence depends on consistency and alignment. When language is disciplined and operationalized, trust increases. When language is abstract or disconnected from practice, satisfaction declines.

Within the LCSM10 framework, leadership language is a governance tool. It is how values are taught, how vision is communicated, how mission is protected, how culture is shaped, how strategy is directed, and how policy is justified.

Learning Outcomes

This chapter was designed to help you understand that organizational alignment is not a leadership preference or philosophical opinion. It is a measurable driver of customer satisfaction, trust, loyalty, and long-term organizational health. You will see how clarity, consistency, and customer-focused leadership language influence real outcomes.

Chapter 3: The LCSM10 Strategic Architecture

A Leadership Model with a Practical Application Framework

This chapter introduces the full LCSM10 framework and explains how its components function together as an integrated leadership system. LCSM10 is not a collection of disconnected statements or leadership ideas, but a comprehensive organizational architecture designed to produce clarity, alignment, and long-term health.

Governing Authority of the LCSM10 Architecture →

The strategic architecture of the LCSM10 is not a neutral leadership model. It is a stewardship framework built under the authority of Scripture and accountable to the standards of God's Word. While this model integrates academic research, organizational theory, and operational discipline, its highest governing authority is biblical truth.

Leadership is not self-authorizing. Strategy is not self-justifying. Governance is not self-legitimizing. All authority is delegated by God and exercised under His accountability.

"There is no power but of God: the powers that be are ordained of God." Romans 13:1 (KJV)

The architecture of values, vision, mission, culture, strategy, and policy is therefore not merely organizational design. It is a moral structure. It is theological stewardship. It is leadership exercised under divine authority.

Within the LCSM10 framework, leaders do not build systems to serve ambition, growth, or influence. They build systems to serve people, protect the mission, preserve integrity, and honor God. Alignment is not pursued solely for efficiency. It is pursued for faithfulness.

"Except the Lord build the house, they labour in vain that build it." Psalm 127:1 (KJV)

This architecture exists to help leaders govern with wisdom, steward with integrity, and lead with accountability before God.

The focus here is on how values, vision, mission, culture, strategy, and policy operate as a unified system rather than as independent initiatives. Each layer supports the next; alignment is intentionally built; and organizational health is sustained through disciplined structure rather than personality-driven leadership. This architecture exists for a specific outcome.

Within the LCSM10, structure is not an end in itself. The framework is designed to protect customer-focused purpose and direction as organizations grow, change, and face pressure. Each component and leadership layer exists to ensure that clarity does not degrade, priorities remain consistent, and customers experience reliability rather than variability. Alignment is the mechanism, but customer trust and satisfaction remain the outcome this architecture is intended to serve.

This chapter positions LCSM10 as a strategic operating framework. It explains how belief becomes behavior, how direction becomes execution, and how purpose is protected through governance. The goal is to provide a clear understanding of how the model works, why each component matters, and how the full architecture produces trust, consistency, and sustainable growth.

Within the LCSM10 framework, this architecture exists for a specific outcome. The purpose of integrating values, vision, mission, culture, strategy, and policy is not merely internal coherence, but the protection of a customer-focused purpose and direction over time. As demonstrated in Lucas (2018), customer satisfaction is influenced when leadership language is clear, disciplined, and consistently reinforced through organizational systems. This chapter establishes how the LCSM10 architecture functions as the structural mechanism that preserves that clarity, ensuring that customer experience remains consistent as organizations grow, change, and face pressure.

The Nine Strategic Components →

The LCSM10 framework is built on nine strategic components that function as the structural anchors of organizational alignment. These components ensure that values, vision, mission, culture, strategy, and policy are developed in an integrated manner. Each component represents a critical dimension of organizational life that must be intentionally defined, aligned, and governed.

Together, these components form the architecture of a healthy organization. They translate leadership language into operational reality and prevent drift by creating clarity across purpose, direction, behavior, execution, and governance.

Each of the nine strategic components functions as a decision lens rather than an internal department or category. Together, they ensure that leadership clarity is evaluated not only by internal coherence but by how effectively purpose, direction, and behavior are experienced by those the organization serves. These components require leaders to consider customer impact, consistency, and trust across every dimension of organizational life, preventing inward focus from replacing service-oriented clarity.

The nine strategic components are:

1. **Customers (Congregants)**
   This component defines who the organization exists to serve. It clarifies the primary audience, their needs, expectations, and experience. Customer clarity shapes mission, informs strategy, guides culture, and determines how success is measured.
2. **Products and Services (Ministries and Services)**
   This component defines what the organization provides. It identifies the core offerings, programs, and services that

fulfill the organization's purpose. A clear definition prevents mission creep and protects focus.

3. Market (Community and Outreach)
   This component defines where the organization serves. It establishes the geographical, cultural, and relational context in which the organization operates and builds trust.
4. Technology and Innovation
   This component defines how the organization adapts and communicates. It governs the tools, systems, and platforms used to support operations, service delivery, and engagement.
5. Sustainability and Growth
   This component defines how the organization remains healthy over time. It addresses financial stewardship, leadership development, resource management, and long-term viability.
6. Core Beliefs and Values
   This component defines what the organization stands for. It establishes the moral, ethical, and theological foundation that governs behavior and decision-making.
7. Self-Identity
   Self-identity does not describe what the organization believes or how it is perceived externally; it describes the role the organization understands itself to occupy in the lives of those it serves.
8. Public Image (Public Perception and Witness)
   This component defines how the organization is experienced externally. It governs reputation, credibility, trust, and community impact.
9. Employees (Support for Staff and Volunteers)
   This component defines how the organization cares for its people. It shapes leadership development, accountability, encouragement, and sustainability.

These nine components ensure that organizational statements are not theoretical. They translate leadership intent into operational structure by requiring that purpose, direction, and governance be constructed comprehensively rather than selectively. When all nine components are present and aligned, clarity becomes sustainable. When one or more components are neglected, drift begins.

Within the LCSM10 framework, these components do not function independently. They work together as a unified system and serve as the required construction lens through which Vision, Mission, and Policy statements are written. Each leadership layer, values, vision, mission, culture, strategy, and policy, is intentionally applied across all nine components, ensuring that customer-focused purpose and direction are expressed consistently rather than shaped by personality or preference.

This is what distinguishes LCSM10 as a leadership system rather than a collection of statements. The framework does not rely on insight alone, but on disciplined construction that produces coherence, alignment, and sustained organizational health.

Component 10 of the LCSM10

The tenth component of the LCSM10 framework is the Alignment Tool. Unlike the nine components, this is not a content element written into the organizational statements. It is a diagnostic and verification mechanism used to evaluate agreement, consistency, and coherence across strategic statements. Alignment answers a foundational question: Do the nine vision components agree with one another, and are they oriented in the same direction, internally or externally?

Within the LCSM10 framework, alignment is evaluated not simply by internal consistency, but by whether the combined direction of the nine components reinforces customer-focused purpose, expectations, and experience.

In its first application, the Alignment Tool is used to evaluate the nine strategic components of the LCSM10 vision framework.

Later, it will be applied across the LCSM10 mission framework. At this stage, its purpose is to determine whether the vision components are complementary rather than contradictory, and whether they consistently direct attention toward those being served rather than inward toward organizational intent.

A vision or mission may include all nine components and still lack alignment if the language, priorities, or assumptions within those components conflict. Misalignment often appears when growth language contradicts sustainability, innovation undermines stated values, or customer focus is weakened by internally centered priorities. The Alignment Tool incorporates scoring disciplines to reveal these tensions by identifying components that are absent, internally focused, externally focused, or inconsistent with declared values.

In addition, the Alignment Tool evaluates how vision language shapes culture. Vision forms expectations for behavior, decision-making, accountability, and leadership conduct. If vision components do not clearly establish how people will be treated and prioritized, culture will form by default rather than by design. This tool ensures that vision functions as a unified, livable framework that aligns focus, values, and culture before it is translated into mission, strategy, and policy.

The Six Leadership Layers

The LCSM10 framework is built on six leadership layers that work together as a single alignment system. These layers represent the progression from belief to behavior, from direction to execution, and from purpose to governance. Each layer builds on the one before it, creating a structure that prevents drift and sustains organizational health.

These layers are not independent initiatives. They are interdependent leadership disciplines. When one layer is weak or neglected, alignment begins to erode. When all six are intentionally developed and consistently reinforced, clarity becomes durable, and trust becomes sustainable. Together, these layers exist to ensure that customer-focused purpose and direction are consistently translated into behavior, decisions, and systems that customers experience as trustworthy and reliable.

These layers are not interchangeable. Values are established first, vision is constructed next, mission follows, culture emerges from consistent leadership behavior, strategy directs execution, and policy protects all that precedes it under pressure.

Values:

Values form the moral and ethical foundation of the organization. They define what the organization stands for and establish the standards by which decisions, behavior, and accountability are governed. Values shape identity and conviction. Without enforced values, leadership credibility weakens, and culture drifts.

Vision:

Vision defines the organization's future direction. It answers where the organization is going and what it is working to become. Vision provides long-term orientation and strategic focus. Without vision, organizations lose direction and operate reactively.

Mission:

A mission defines the organization's present purpose. It answers why the organization exists and who it serves. Mission governs daily priorities, decision-making, and behavior. Without mission clarity, organizations lose focus and coherence.

Culture:

Culture is the lived expression of leadership. It reflects how values, vision, and mission are put into practice every day. Culture determines what is rewarded, tolerated, and expected. Without intentional culture formation, habits replace conviction, and drift becomes normalized.

Strategy:

Strategy provides disciplined movement toward the vision. It defines priorities, allocates resources, and guides execution. Strategy turns direction into action. Without a strategy, vision becomes ambition without progress.

Policy:

Policy protects the organization from drift. It establishes boundaries, accountability, and governance. Policy ensures that values, culture, and strategy are sustained under pressure. Without purposeful policy, standards erode, and leadership authority weakens.

Together, these six layers form a complete leadership operating system. Values define belief. Vision defines direction. Mission defines purpose. Culture defines behavior. Strategy defines movement. Policy defines protection. Within the LCSM10 framework, alignment occurs when all six layers function together across the nine strategic components. This is what transforms leadership language into organizational reality.

When the strategic components and leadership layers are integrated, alignment emerges not as an initiative to manage, but as the underlying structure that holds customer-focused purpose and direction together.

Alignment As Infrastructure

Alignment is not a leadership initiative. It is organizational infrastructure. Just as a building depends on a stable foundation, load-bearing walls, and reliable systems, a healthy organization depends on alignment between its values, vision, mission, culture, strategy, and policy. When these elements are integrated and reinforced, the organization becomes structurally sound. When they are disconnected, the organization becomes vulnerable to drift, instability, and collapse under pressure. Like physical infrastructure, alignment requires ongoing leadership attention; without reinforcement, maintenance, and repair, even well-designed systems deteriorate over time.

Infrastructure is rarely visible, but it determines everything. Customers do not see governance systems. Staff do not always recognize leadership architecture. Stakeholders may never read policy documents. Yet every decision, every interaction, every service experience is shaped by the strength or weakness of what exists beneath the surface. Alignment functions the same way: It supports clarity. It sustains trust. It protects culture. It stabilizes strategy. It reinforces accountability.

When alignment is treated as infrastructure, leadership becomes intentional rather than reactive. Decision-making becomes consistent rather than situational. Growth becomes sustainable rather than chaotic. Culture becomes principled rather than personality-driven.

Within the LCSM10 framework, alignment is designed, built, and maintained. It is not assumed. It is not accidental. It is constructed through disciplined leadership language, enforced values, clear vision, practiced mission, formed culture, executed strategy, and purposeful policy.

Organizations do not drift because they lack passion. They drift because their infrastructure is weak.

Alignment is the structure that holds everything together.

Leadership As Culture Architect

Culture does not form by accident. It is built, shaped, and sustained by leadership. Every organization has a culture, whether it is intentional or unmanaged. The difference lies in whether leaders design it or simply inherit it. Culture reflects what is rewarded, tolerated, corrected, and ignored. It is expressed through daily behavior, decision-making, communication, and accountability. Over time, these patterns become the organization's identity.

Leadership is the primary architect of culture. What leaders model becomes normalized. What leaders enforce becomes standard. What leaders overlook becomes acceptable. Teams watch leadership closely, not only for what is said, but for what is done under pressure. Values printed on walls matter far less than values demonstrated in difficult decisions. Over time, this leadership-shaped culture becomes visible to those the organization serves, influencing how customers experience consistency, care, accountability, and trust in every interaction.

When leaders take responsibility for culture, they shape an environment where purpose is practiced, standards are clear, and trust is reinforced. When leaders avoid culture formation, habits replace intention, convenience replaces conviction, and drift becomes embedded.

Within the LCSM10 framework, culture is the bridge between belief and behavior. Values define what matters. Vision defines where the organization is going. Mission defines why it exists. Culture determines whether those commitments are lived.

Leadership does not merely influence culture. Leadership creates it.

Why Systems Matter

It is not the lack of individual talent that leads to organizational failure. Organizations fail because of the systems that shape behavior, guide decisions, and reinforce priorities. Systems determine what gets done, how it gets done, and whether it is done consistently. Hiring, training, communication, decision-making, budgeting, accountability, and governance form the operational backbone of the organization. When these systems are aligned with values, vision, and mission, they create clarity and stability. When they are disconnected, confusion and inconsistency follow.

Strong systems reduce dependence on personality-driven leadership. They make expectations clear, standardize best practices, and protect culture under pressure. They ensure that purpose is not dependent on who happens to be in the room.

Weak systems create vulnerability. Good intentions are undermined by poor execution. Leaders compensate for structural gaps with personal effort. Over time, fatigue replaces focus, and drift becomes normalized.

PART II

THE SIX LEADERSHIP LAYERS

This section introduces the six leadership layers that form the operational core of the LCSM10 framework. These layers represent the progression from belief to behavior, from customer-focused purpose to execution, and from direction to governance. Together, they establish the structural conditions required to sustain clarity, consistency, and trust over time.

This is where values, vision, and mission are examined as leadership disciplines and integrated into a unified system. Each layer builds upon the one before it, ensuring that purpose and direction are not only defined but reinforced through culture, strategy, and policy. These chapters demonstrate how leadership language becomes organizational reality and how alignment is intentionally constructed rather than assumed.

Chapter 4
LAYER ONE: VALUES

The Moral and Ethical Foundation of Leadership →

This chapter establishes values as the moral and ethical foundation of leadership and the governing authority within the LCSM10 framework. Values define what is right, true, and honorable before God, and they determine how leaders think, decide, and act, especially under pressure. They serve as the organization's conscience, shaping conduct when observation is absent and accountability is minimal.

Scripture teaches that leadership without a firm foundation cannot endure. In the same way, organizations built without clearly defined and faithfully enforced values may appear successful for a season but lack the integrity required for longevity. Vision may inspire, strategy may organize, and policy may govern, but values determine whether leadership is trustworthy, authority is exercised faithfully, and influence is worthy of stewardship.

Within the LCSM10 framework, values are not optional ideals or abstract commitments. They govern convictions, establish decision boundaries, and define the standards by which leadership behavior is evaluated. When values are clear and consistently enforced, leadership credibility strengthens, culture stabilizes, and trust grows. When values are neglected or inconsistently applied, every other leadership layer becomes unstable.

This chapter establishes that values are not optional ideals. They govern convictions. They must be rooted in truth, reflected in behavior, and enforced with integrity. When values are clear and consistently lived out, leadership is strengthened, culture is protected, and trust is built.

What Values Really Are

Values are not slogans, branding statements, or aspirational ideals. They govern convictions. They define what an organization believes is right, true, and worth defending. Values shape identity, guide decisions, and establish the boundaries of acceptable behavior. They function as the moral compass of leadership and the conscience of the organization.

Values are foundational commitments that inform every other leadership layer. They are not created for appearance. They exist for accountability. Values determine how people are treated, how problems are handled, how resources are stewarded, and how pressure is managed. When leaders face difficult choices, values are the standard by which those choices are measured.

Biblically, values reflect obedience to God's truth. Scripture teaches that righteousness exalts a nation and that integrity guards the soul. In the same way, values define an organization's character. They shape whether leadership is trustworthy, whether culture is healthy, and whether influence is honorable.

Values are also relational. They govern how leaders serve others, how authority is exercised, and how responsibility is carried. When values are clear and consistently practiced, people experience stability, fairness, and trust. When values are vague or inconsistently applied, confusion and cynicism take root.

Within the LCSM10 framework, values are the root system of leadership. Vision grows from values. Mission flows from values. Culture reflects values. Strategy must honor values. Policy must protect values. When values are clearly defined and faithfully enforced, alignment becomes possible. When values are neglected, everything else becomes unstable. Values are not what an organization says it believes. Values are what an organization demonstrates it believes in through its actions.

Biblical Foundation of Values

Biblical values are not philosophical ideals or cultural preferences. They are rooted in the revealed character of God and the authority of Scripture. From the beginning, God established that life, leadership, and community are governed by truth, righteousness, justice, mercy, and obedience. These values are not optional. They are the foundation upon which faithful leadership is built.

Scripture teaches that a life, a household, and a nation are only as strong as the values that govern them.

"Righteousness exalts a nation, but sin is a reproach to any people." Proverbs 14:34 (ESV)

"The integrity of the upright guides them, but the crookedness of the treacherous destroys them." Proverbs 11:3 (ESV)

Values determine direction. They shape decisions long before circumstances demand them. They establish the standard by which leaders measure success and evaluate behavior. Jesus taught that obedience to God's truth is the mark of wisdom.

"Everyone then who hears these words of mine and does them will be like a wise man who built his house on the rock." Matthew 7:24 (ESV)

Leadership that is not grounded in God's truth may appear successful for a season, but it lacks the foundation to endure pressure, opposition, and adversity. Biblical values begin with the fear of the Lord, which Scripture identifies as the starting point of wisdom.

"The fear of the Lord is the beginning of wisdom, and the knowledge of the Holy One is insight." Proverbs 9:10 (ESV)

The fear of the Lord is not terror. It is reverence. It is submission. It is recognition that God alone defines what is right, what is good, and what is worthy of obedience. Throughout Scripture, God evaluates leaders not by their accomplishments but by their faithfulness.

"He has told you, O man, what is good; and what does the Lord require of you but to do justice, and to love kindness, and to walk humbly with your God?" Micah 6:8 (ESV)

Biblical leadership is measured by character before results. Authority is not granted for personal ambition. It is entrusted for stewardship.

"Moreover, it is required of stewards that they be found faithful." 1 Corinthians 4:2 (ESV)

Leaders are not owners. They are caretakers. Influence is not possessed. It is entrusted. Scripture teaches that leadership is a sacred responsibility and that those who lead will give an account. "Obey your leaders and submit to them, for they are keeping watch over your souls, as those who will have to give an account." Hebrews 13:17 (ESV)

Biblical values also establish how authority is exercised. Leadership is not domination. It is a service.

"Whoever would be great among you must be your servant." Mark 10:43 (ESV)

Power without righteousness leads to corruption. Authority without humility leads to pride. Success without obedience leads to destruction.

These biblical principles are not presented solely as moral encouragement. Within the LCSM10 framework, they function as governing standards that must be translated into leadership expectations, behavioral boundaries, and accountability systems. Scripture establishes what God requires of leaders; values determine how those requirements are enforced within organizational life. When biblical truth is not embedded into leadership structure, it remains inspirational rather than operational. Faithful leadership requires that what God commands be protected through discipline, correction, and consistency, not intention alone.

When leadership is rooted in biblical values, organizations are built on truth, guided by wisdom, and sustained by integrity. When leadership is disconnected from biblical values, no amount of strategy, structure, or policy can prevent drift. A foundation built on anything else will not endure.

Values As Decision Filters

Every leader makes hundreds of decisions each week. Some are small. Others carry lasting consequences. In moments of pressure, uncertainty, or conflict, leaders do not rise to their best intentions. They fall back on their deepest convictions. That is why values must function as decision filters rather than decorative statements. Decision filters govern choices before action occurs; behavioral boundaries govern conduct after decisions are made.

A decision filter is a standard that governs choice. It clarifies what is acceptable, honorable, and faithful. When values are clearly defined and consistently enforced, they become the lens through which every decision is evaluated. They determine not only what leaders can do, but what they should do.

Biblically, decision-making is never separated from obedience.

"Trust in the Lord with all your heart, and do not lean on your own understanding. In all your ways acknowledge him, and he will make straight your paths." Proverbs 3:5–6 (ESV)

Scripture teaches that wisdom flows from submission to God's truth. Leaders are called to seek His will before pursuing opportunity, profit, or popularity.

"When wisdom enters your heart, and knowledge is pleasant to your soul, discretion will watch over you, understanding will guard you." Proverbs 2:10–11 (ESV)

Values serve this same function within leadership. They guard discretion. They shape judgment. They prevent compromise. When a decision aligns with stated values, leaders can move forward with confidence. When a decision violates those values, it must be rejected regardless of convenience or gain.

Without values as filters, decisions become situational. Ethics becomes flexible. Standards bend under pressure. What is right today becomes optional tomorrow. Over time, compromise accumulates, and drift becomes normalized.

Jesus warned that divided loyalty produces instability.

"No one can serve two masters." Matthew 6:24 (ESV)

Leadership without clear values is leadership without a master. It becomes driven by urgency, emotion, or ambition rather than truth.

Within the LCSM10 framework, values function as the first gate every decision must pass through. Strategy must honor values. Culture must reflect values. Policy must protect values. Vision must be pursued within values. Mission must be executed through values.

When values serve as decision filters, leadership gains clarity, credibility, and consistency. When values are ignored, leadership loses authority, and trust erodes. Values do not make decisions easier; however, they do help make the right decisions.

Values As Behavioral Boundaries

Values do more than guide decisions. They establish boundaries for behavior. They define what is acceptable, what is honorable, and what will not be tolerated. In this way, values function as guardrails that protect the organization from drift, compromise, and ethical erosion.

Boundaries are not restrictive. They are protective. Scripture teaches that God's commands are given for our good, not our harm. In the same way, organizational values are designed to preserve integrity, trust, and unity.

"I will set no worthless thing before my eyes." Psalm 101:3 (ESV)

This is the language of boundaries. It is a declaration that certain behaviors, attitudes, and actions are incompatible with faithful leadership. When values are clearly defined, leaders know where the line is drawn. Staff know what is expected. Customers know what the organization stands for. Conflict is resolved more quickly because standards are shared. Accountability becomes fair because expectations are clear. Biblical Leadership Requires Discipline.

"Do not be conformed to this world, but be transformed by the renewal of your mind." Romans 12:2 (ESV)

Transformation requires separation from what corrupts. Values establish that separation. They identify the conduct that honors God and the conduct that undermines witness. Without behavioral boundaries, culture becomes permissive. Standards erode. Inconsistency grows. What was once unthinkable becomes acceptable. Over time, the organization drifts from its calling and compromises its testimony.

Scripture Warns Against Leadership Without Restraint.

"Where there is no vision, the people cast off restraint." Proverbs 29:18 (ESV)

Values provide restraint. They anchor conduct. They define the moral perimeter of leadership.

Within the LCSM10 framework, values establish the behavioral limits that protect mission, preserve culture, and safeguard trust. They define how authority is exercised, how conflict is handled, how resources are stewarded, and how pressure is faced.

When values function as behavioral boundaries, leadership gains credibility and culture gains stability. When boundaries are ignored, drift accelerates, and integrity is lost. Values do not merely inspire behavior. They govern it.

Values As Leadership Accountability →

Accountability is the mechanism by which values move from stated conviction to enforceable leadership obligation. Values are not only personal convictions. They are leadership obligations. When a leader affirms a set of values, those values become a public commitment. They establish the standard by which leadership behavior will be evaluated and trusted.

Accountability begins with alignment between what leaders say and what they do. When leadership behavior reflects stated values, credibility is built. When leadership behavior contradicts stated values, trust erodes. Over time, people stop listening to what leaders say and start watching what leaders tolerate.

Values define the line of responsibility. They clarify what leaders are willing to defend, correct, and enforce. They establish the moral authority of leadership. Without accountability, values become symbolic. With accountability, values become operational.

Leadership accountability requires consistency. Values must govern:

- Hiring decisions
- Promotions and terminations
- Conflict resolution
- Financial stewardship
- Customer treatment
- Staff development
- Discipline and restoration

Accountability is not punishment. It is protection. It protects the organization from drift. It protects people from unfair treatment. It protects leadership from ethical compromise. It protects the mission from reputational damage.

Within the LCSM10 framework, values establish the accountability standard for every other leadership layer. Vision must be pursued with integrity. The mission must be executed with faithfulness. Culture must reflect character. Strategy must honor convictions. Policy must protect principles.

Leadership without accountability produces hypocrisy. Leadership with accountability produces trust. Values are the standard by which leadership is judged.

Why Values Fail When Not Enforced

Values fail when they are treated as statements rather than standards. An organization may publish a list of values, display them on walls, and reference them in meetings, yet if leadership does not consistently enforce them, those values lose authority. Over time, they become symbolic language rather than operational truth.

Enforcement is what gives values credibility. When leaders confront behavior that violates stated values, they communicate that those values matter. When leaders overlook violations, they communicate that values are optional. People quickly learn which standards are real and which are merely aspirational.

Selective enforcement is especially damaging. When values are applied to some people but not others, trust collapses. High performers become cynical. Emerging leaders become confused. Culture fractures into personal interpretations rather than shared convictions.

Values also fail when they are disconnected from leadership systems. Hiring, onboarding, performance reviews, promotion decisions, discipline, and termination must all reflect stated values. If systems reward results without regard for conduct, values will always lose.

Over time, unenforced values create cultural drift. Standards erode. Expectations blur. Behavior becomes personality-driven rather than principle-driven. The organization may still speak about its values, but no longer lives by them.

Within the LCSM10 framework, values only function when they are enforced through leadership behavior and organizational systems. Values that are protected become culture. Values that are ignored become decoration. Values fail when leaders tolerate what they claim to oppose. At that point, failure is no longer a matter of leadership inconsistency alone, but evidence of systems that reward outcomes without regard for conduct and permit drift to persist unchallenged.

How Values Shape Culture

Culture is the visible expression of values in action. It is what people experience every day in how decisions are made, how problems are handled, how authority is exercised, and how people are treated. While values define what an organization believes, culture reveals what an organization actually practices.

Values shape culture by setting the standards that govern behavior. When values are clearly defined and consistently enforced, they establish shared expectations. People know what is right, what is acceptable, and what is honored. Over time, these standards become habits. Those habits become norms. Those norms become culture.

Leaders shape culture through what they reward, what they correct, and what they tolerate. When leaders promote people who embody the organization's values, those values become aspirational. When leaders confront behavior that violates those values, those values become protected. When leaders overlook violations, those values become optional.

Culture is formed in moments of pressure. How leaders respond to conflict, failure, growth, and crisis communicates more about values than any written statement. In those moments, people learn what truly matters and what does not.

When values are lived out consistently, culture becomes stable and trustworthy. When values are applied selectively, culture becomes fragmented and unpredictable. When values are ignored, culture becomes personality-driven rather than principle-driven.

Within the LCSM10 framework, culture is the lived expression of values. Values define the moral and ethical foundation. Culture is the daily reality built upon that foundation. When values are clear and enforced, culture becomes strong. When values are neglected, culture becomes fragile. Culture does not reveal what leaders say they believe. Culture reveals what leaders are willing to defend.

Values Under Pressure

Values are revealed most clearly under pressure. In calm seasons, it is easy for organizations to speak about integrity, humility, excellence, and service. In difficult seasons, those same values are tested. Pressure exposes whether values are convictions or conveniences.

When resources are tight, values determine whether leaders cut corners or steward faithfully. When conflict arises, values determine whether leaders pursue truth and reconciliation or protect their reputation. When growth accelerates, values determine whether people are treated as partners or as tools. When crisis strikes, values determine whether leaders respond with courage or retreat into self-preservation. Pressure does not create character. It reveals it.

Leaders often believe their values are strong until they face competing priorities. Time constraints, financial strain, public scrutiny, and organizational conflict all force choices. In those moments, values become either anchors or obstacles. Anchors hold leadership steady. Obstacles are discarded.

Organizations drift when leaders treat values as ideals that apply only when conditions are favorable. Faithful leadership applies values when they are costly. That is when credibility is built. That is when trust is formed. That is when culture is shaped.

People watch leadership closely during pressure. They observe who is protected, who is blamed, who is rewarded, and who is sacrificed. Those moments teach more about values than any training session or policy manual.

Within the LCSM10 framework, values are designed to endure pressure, not avoid it. They exist to guide leadership when decisions are difficult, when tradeoffs are painful, and when obedience requires sacrifice. Pressure does not weaken values. It proves them.

From Values to Vision

Values define what an organization believes and what it is willing to defend. They establish the moral authority of leadership and the boundaries within which all decisions must be made. But values alone do not provide direction. They tell leaders what is right, not where to go.

Without vision, even well-intentioned organizations can become stagnant, reactive, or internally focused. Values ensure faithfulness. Vision provides focus. Values guard integrity. Vision establishes direction. Leadership requires both.

Within the LCSM10 framework, vision is not developed apart from values. It grows out of them. Vision translates conviction into direction and belief into purpose. Once values are clear and enforced, leadership is prepared to answer the next essential question: Where is God calling this organization to go, and whom is it being called to serve?

Before You Write Your Values →

You are preparing to define the moral and ethical foundation of your organization. This work is not symbolic, aspirational, or branding language. The values you will write are meant to become the governing convictions of your leadership, your culture, your strategy, and your policy.

This book is designed first to establish the leadership framework, biblical foundation, and research-based architecture of organizational alignment. The practical work of discovering, evaluating, and writing your value statements is intentionally placed in the workbook section at the end of this book. That section is where you will move from understanding to application. It is where conviction becomes structure, belief becomes behavior, and intention becomes governance. The values you write will define what your organization defends. They will determine what leaders correct. They will establish what behavior is tolerated. They will shape how authority is exercised. They will govern how people are treated.

When you reach the workbook section, you will not be drafting ideas. You will build standards that guide decisions, protect integrity, and anchor your organization's future. These values will not describe who you hope to be. They will declare who you are committed to becoming.

Once written, your values will become a public commitment. They will be tested under pressure. They will be examined in moments of conflict. Your behavior will measure them.

This is not a creative exercise. It is a leadership responsibility. Write with clarity. Write with conviction. Write with integrity. You are not defining what your organization hopes to be. You are defining what it will stand for.

Chapter 5
LAYER TWO: VISION

Define Organizational Destination

Vision establishes the future that an organization is committed to pursuing. It defines the destination leadership is responsible for reaching, and the outcome that the organization exists to deliver to the people it serves. Vision is not imagination or aspiration. It is a direction.

Within the LCSM10 framework, vision functions as a governing leadership construct. It translates values into forward movement and provides a clear reference point for decision-making, resource allocation, cultural development, and long-term planning. Vision answers the question of where the organization is going and why that destination matters.

When vision is clear, externally focused, and aligned with values, it becomes a unifying force that drives mission, shapes culture, informs strategy, and anchors policy. When vision is vague, internally focused, or disconnected from operations, organizations drift, lose momentum, and fracture under pressure.

The purpose of this chapter is to establish vision as a leadership discipline, not a creative exercise. Vision defines the future that future leadership is responsible for building.

What Vision Is And Is Not

Vision is the clear, future-focused picture of where an organization is going and what it is ultimately becoming. It defines destination rather than activity. Vision answers the question, "Where are we going?" and provides leaders and teams with a shared horizon that guides decisions, priorities, and long-term investment.

Vision is not a slogan or a marketing phrase. It is not a collection of inspirational words designed to stir emotion without providing direction. Vision is not a list of goals, programs, or tactics, and it does not describe what the organization does each day. Instead, vision defines what the organization is becoming over time.

A true vision statement is directional rather than operational. It establishes a fixed destination that remains stable even as strategies change. Programs may evolve, methods may shift, markets may change, and technology may advance, but vision remains anchored. It serves as the long-term reference point that keeps leadership aligned and focused beyond short-term pressures.

Vision is also not a personal ambition. It is not the dream of a single leader imposed on others. It is a shared picture of the future that reflects the organization's values, purpose, and responsibility. When vision is properly formed, it unifies leadership, aligns teams, and provides a standard for evaluating every major decision.

Vision gives meaning to effort by connecting present work to future impact. It explains why sacrifice is required, justifies long-term discipline, and creates continuity between daily action and enduring purpose.

Vision Versus Ambition

Vision and ambition are often confused, yet they are fundamentally different in purpose, scope, and effect. Ambition is driven by personal desire, recognition, power, or achievement. It centers on what a leader wants to accomplish for themselves or their legacy. Vision, by contrast, is anchored in responsibility. It is oriented toward what an organization is called to become in service to others and in fulfillment of its purpose.

Ambition focuses on position. Vision focuses on the destination. Ambition seeks advancement, influence, and control. Vision seeks direction, stewardship, and long-term impact. Ambition asks, "How far can I go?" Vision asks, "Where must we go, and whom are we called to serve along the way?"

Ambition is often short-term and reactive, shaped by competition, pressure, and opportunity. Vision is long-term and deliberate, shaped by values, mission, and conviction. Ambition can change with circumstances, markets, or leadership transitions. Vision remains stable, providing continuity even when leadership changes or external conditions shift.

Ambition may inspire effort, but it rarely sustains sacrifice. Vision creates endurance. Ambition may motivate activity, but vision gives it meaning. Ambition can drive growth, but vision determines whether that growth is healthy, sustainable, and aligned with purpose.

When ambition leads, organizations often chase success without direction. When vision leads, organizations pursue progress with clarity and integrity. A vision-centered organization measures success not only by what it achieves, but by what it becomes.

Biblical Models of Vision

Scripture presents vision as God-given direction that shapes leadership, unifies people, and anchors action in obedience rather than impulse. Biblical vision is not human imagination projected onto the future. It is discerned through prayer, revelation, and faithful stewardship of God's calling. Throughout Scripture, vision consistently precedes movement, reform, restoration, and growth.

The Bible is explicit about the consequences of visionlessness.

Proverbs 29:18 declares, "Where there is no vision, the people perish: but he that keepeth the law, happy is he" (KJV). The word translated as vision refers to divine revelation and moral direction. When vision is absent, restraint is cast off, discipline erodes, and leadership collapses into reaction rather than direction. When vision is present, people are anchored in truth, ordered toward God's purposes, and protected from drift.

In the Old Testament, vision is repeatedly associated with clarity of purpose and obedience to God's will. God's calling of Abraham illustrates vision as a forward-looking destination rooted in promise. In Genesis 12, God called Abraham to leave his homeland and go to a place He would show him. Abraham was not given a tactical plan. He was given a destination and a promise. His obedience was anchored in trust, not certainty. Vision did not remove risk. It gave meaning to obedience.

Moses demonstrates vision as covenant direction. God did not simply deliver Israel from Egypt. He gave them a destination, the Promised Land, and a covenant identity. Moses repeatedly reminded the people not only where they were going, but who they were becoming as God's chosen people. Vision shaped their laws, worship, culture, and national identity.

Nehemiah provides one of the clearest models of organizational vision in Scripture. When he returned to Jerusalem, he did not begin with construction. He began with an assessment. He surveyed the broken walls, discerned God's call, and then presented a clear vision to the people. He named the problem, declared the destination, and invited the people into a shared future. The result was unified action, sacrificial commitment, and restoration of the city.

In the New Testament, Jesus embodies the ultimate model of vision. He did not merely teach morality. He proclaimed the Kingdom of God and invited His followers into a new identity, a new purpose, and a new future. His vision was not limited to individual salvation. It was the restoration of all things under the reign of God. Every parable, miracle, and command pointed toward that destination.

The apostle Paul carried this vision forward. He described the church as the body of Christ, called to maturity, unity, and faithful witness. His letters consistently pointed believers beyond present struggle toward future glory, reminding them that their labor was not in vain because it was anchored in an eternal vision.

Biblical vision is therefore not about personal success, institutional growth, or human achievement. It is about alignment with God's purposes. It is about stewarding influence faithfully. It is about leading people toward the future God intends rather than the future culture demands. When leadership is anchored in biblical vision, direction becomes clear, sacrifice becomes meaningful, and obedience becomes faithful.

Vision As Strategic Direction →

Vision functions as the strategic direction of an organization. It establishes the destination toward which every decision, investment, and initiative must move. Strategy determines how the organization will move. Vision determines where it is going. Without a clear vision, strategy becomes fragmented, reactive, and short-sighted. With a clear vision, strategy becomes focused, disciplined, and aligned.

Quarterly objectives or annual plans do not define strategic direction. It is defined by a long-range understanding of what the organization is becoming and why it exists. Vision provides the fixed point on the horizon that allows leaders to evaluate opportunities, allocate resources, and prioritize initiatives with clarity and confidence. It becomes the reference point for determining what belongs in the future and what does not.

Within the LCSM10 framework, vision serves as the directional anchor for every other leadership layer. Values define the moral foundation. Vision defines the future destination. Mission defines daily purpose. Culture defines the lived environment. Strategy defines the path forward. Policy protects alignment. When vision is absent or unclear, each of these layers operates independently, producing confusion and misalignment. When vision is clear, the entire organization moves with unity and purpose.

Strategic direction requires long-term thinking. Leaders must be willing to look beyond immediate pressures, short-term gains, and reactive decision-making. Vision allows leaders to invest today for outcomes that may not be fully realized for years. It justifies patience, discipline, and perseverance. It gives meaning to sacrifice and endurance.

Vision also functions as a decision filter. Every major initiative must be tested against the destination. Leaders must be able to answer whether a proposal moves the organization closer to its future or distracts it from its calling. When vision governs decision-making, growth becomes intentional rather than accidental, and progress becomes measurable rather than assumed.

In effective organizations, vision stabilizes leadership during seasons of change. Markets shift. Technology advances. Competition increases. Economic conditions fluctuate. Vision remains constant. It provides continuity when methods must adapt. It allows organizations to evolve without losing identity.

Vision as strategic direction is not about predicting the future. It is about preparing for it. It is about defining the future God is calling the organization to steward and then aligning every layer of leadership to move faithfully toward that destination.

Vision As Leadership Responsibility

Vision is a leadership responsibility. It is not delegated to committees, outsourced to consultants, or discovered through consensus alone. Vision originates with leadership because leadership is accountable for direction. Those entrusted with authority are responsible for the organization's future.

Throughout Scripture, God holds leaders responsible for the direction of His people. When leaders failed to seek God's direction, the people suffered. When leaders walked in obedience and clarity, the people flourished. Vision is not optional for leadership. It is a sacred duty.

Leaders are called to see what others cannot yet see. They must discern where the organization is being led, not merely manage where it currently stands. Vision requires prayer, humility, discernment, and courage. It demands that leaders listen for God's direction, weigh responsibility carefully, and then speak with clarity and conviction.

Biblically, leadership vision is not rooted in personal ambition or self-promotion. It is rooted in stewardship. Leaders do not own the organization. They serve it. They do not use vision to build personal platforms. They use vision to guide God's people and resources toward His purposes faithfully.

Moses did not choose Israel's destination. God revealed it. Nehemiah did not invent Jerusalem's future. He discerned it through prayer and obedience. Joshua did not lead by popularity. He led by conviction. Each leader carried the responsibility of direction before they carried the responsibility of management.

Vision also requires moral courage. Leaders must be willing to stand alone before they can lead together. They must be willing to speak the truth when silence would be safer. They must be willing to pursue God's calling even when resistance arises. Vision is often costly before it is celebrated.

Within the LCSM10 framework, vision is not a team exercise detached from leadership authority. It is a leadership mandate that must then be stewarded, communicated, protected, and carried throughout the organization. When leaders abdicate vision, organizations drift. When leaders own a vision, organizations move with purpose.

Vision is not discovered accidentally. It is discerned deliberately. It is shaped through prayer, Scripture, responsibility, and obedience. Leadership is measured not only by how well it manages today, but by how faithfully it prepares for tomorrow.

Vision Is The Burden Leaders Carry For The Future →

Vision is the burden leaders carry for the future. It is not a casual idea or a passing thought. It is a weight that settles on the heart and will not let go. True vision does not simply inspire. It compels. It presses. It disrupts comfort and demands a response.

Nehemiah is a clear biblical model of this kind of vision. When news reached him that Jerusalem's walls were broken down and its gates burned with fire, the condition of God's city pierced his heart. Scripture records that he did not respond with indifference or mild concern. He wept. He mourned. He fasted. He prayed. The condition of the city became a personal burden that he could not ignore.

Nehemiah 1:3–4 (ESV) records, "And they said to me, 'The remnant there in the province who had survived the exile is in great trouble and shame. The wall of Jerusalem is broken down, and its gates are destroyed by fire.' As soon as I heard these words, I sat down and wept and mourned for days, and I continued fasting and praying before the God of heaven."

This was not strategic planning. This was not an organizational assessment. This was vision forming in the heart of a leader. The future of Jerusalem became a weight Nehemiah carried in prayer. He was not even living in the city. He was serving as cupbearer to the king. Yet God placed the burden of rebuilding on his heart.

That burden did not fade with time. It deepened. It followed him into the king's presence. It eventually became visible on his face. When the king noticed Nehemiah's sorrow, Nehemiah stood at a crossroads. He could have hidden his grief and returned to comfort, or he could have carried the burden forward in faith.

Nehemiah 2:2–3 (ESV) records, "And the king said to me, 'Why is your face sad, seeing you are not sick? This is nothing but sadness of the heart.' Then I was very much afraid. I said to the king, 'Let the king live forever! Why should not my face be sad, when the city, the place of my fathers' graves, lies in ruins, and its gates have been destroyed by fire?'"

This is the moment vision becomes leadership. Nehemiah did not simply feel compassion. He spoke with conviction. He did not remain silent. He carried the burden into action. His vision moved from prayer to responsibility.

Nehemiah's vision was not personal ambition. It was not career advancement. It was not self-promotion. It was obedience to a burden God placed on his heart. That burden cost him comfort, safety, and security. Yet it also positioned him to lead one of the greatest rebuilding efforts in biblical history.

Vision always begins this way. It begins with a burden. It begins with seeing what is broken and feeling responsible for rebuilding it. It begins with tears before it begins with plans. It begins with prayer before moving into action.

Leaders do not choose their burdens. God gives them. Some burdens are for people. Some are for communities. Some are for institutions. Some are for generations yet to be born. The weight of vision is what distinguishes leadership from management.

Nehemiah carried the future of Jerusalem in his heart before he ever carried a brick in his hands. That is the nature of vision. It becomes a responsibility leaders cannot escape. It is the burden they carry for the future God has entrusted to them.

Why Vision Erodes

Vision erodes when leaders stop guarding it. Vision is not self-sustaining. It requires continual reinforcement, disciplined alignment, and courageous protection. When leaders assume that vision will remain clear without intentional stewardship, it slowly fades into memory, tradition, or rhetoric. Over time, organizations continue operating, but they no longer move toward a defined future. They remain busy without being directed.

Vision also erodes when urgency replaces direction. Daily pressure, operational demands, financial stress, and personnel issues pull leadership's attention toward immediate needs. When leaders spend all their energy solving today's problems without returning to tomorrow's destination, the organization becomes reactive. Short-term survival replaces long-term purpose. Decisions begin to prioritize convenience over direction, and the future slowly disappears from view.

Vision erodes when leadership changes without transfer. When a founder, pastor, or executive carries the vision personally but fails to embed it institutionally, the vision leaves when the leader leaves. New leadership may bring competence and skill, but without a clear handoff of direction, the organization resets itself around new priorities, new preferences, or new ambitions. Continuity is lost, and momentum stalls.

Vision erodes when culture contradicts direction. If behavior, incentives, and systems do not reinforce the stated vision, people stop believing it. What leaders reward becomes more influential than what leaders say. When promotions, recognition, and resources flow toward short-term results rather than long-term direction, the vision becomes symbolic rather than governing.

Vision also erodes when fear replaces faith. Leaders who fear conflict, resistance, or loss of approval often soften the vision to avoid tension. Over time, vision becomes diluted, compromised, and negotiated until it no longer carries authority. What once required courage becomes optional. What once demanded sacrifice becomes inconvenient.

Organizations rarely abandon vision deliberately. They lose it gradually; erosion is subtle. It feels practical. It feels responsible. It feels necessary. Yet over time, drift erodes clarity, weakens alignment, and leaves organizations moving without purpose. Vision must be guarded, or it will be lost.

How Vision Unifies Organizations →

Vision unifies organizations by providing a shared destination that transcends individual roles, preferences, and ambitions. When leaders articulate a clear and compelling picture of the future, they provide a common horizon that aligns effort, priorities, and decision-making across every level of the organization. Vision answers the question of where the organization is going, and when that destination is understood, people can move together with purpose rather than in competing directions.

Vision creates unity by establishing a common reason for sacrifice. Growth, change, and transformation require effort, discipline, and at times discomfort. When people understand the destination, they are more willing to endure the cost of the journey.

Vision explains why hard work matters, why patience is required, and why perseverance is necessary. It connects present labor to future impact and gives meaning to daily responsibility.

Vision also unifies by providing a standard for decision-making. When leaders and teams face competing priorities, limited resources, or difficult trade-offs, vision serves as the reference point. Decisions are no longer driven by personal preference or departmental interest but by what best serves the organization's future direction. This creates alignment across departments, ministries, and teams because everyone is measuring success by the same destination.

Vision unifies leadership. When senior leaders share the same picture of the future, they lead with coherence rather than contradiction. Strategy becomes coordinated. Communication becomes consistent. Expectations become clear. Teams gain confidence because they are not receiving mixed signals about where the organization is headed.

Vision also unifies culture. Over time, shared direction shapes shared language, shared values, and shared identity. People begin to speak about the organization's future with ownership rather than detachment. The vision becomes part of how the organization understands itself. This creates stability, continuity, and trust.

Unity does not come from structure alone. It comes from shared direction. When vision is clear, people move together. When vision is absent, people move independently. A unified organization is not one without disagreement, but one that is committed to the same destination.

Vision As A Filter For Opportunity

Every organization is surrounded by opportunity. New partnerships, new markets, new programs, new technologies, and new revenue streams constantly present themselves as potential paths forward. Not every opportunity, however, is the right opportunity. Without a clear vision, leaders are left to evaluate opportunities based on urgency, emotion, financial pressure, or short-term gain rather than long-term direction.

Vision functions as a filter that protects the organization from distraction. It provides a standard against which every opportunity must be measured. The question is not whether an opportunity is good, profitable, popular, or impressive. The question is whether it moves the organization closer to its destination. Vision allows leaders to say yes with confidence and no with clarity.

When vision is absent, organizations become reactive. They chase trends, follow competitors, and pursue every open door. Over time, resources become fragmented, focus is diluted, and momentum is lost. What appears to be expansion becomes exhaustion. Opportunity without direction eventually leads to confusion.

Vision brings discipline to decision-making. It enables leaders to evaluate opportunities through the lens of purpose, identity, and long-term impact. A vision-centered organization does not reject opportunity. It selects an opportunity. It chooses paths that reinforce its calling rather than compete with it.

Vision also protects culture. New opportunities often introduce new people, new pressures, and new expectations. When those opportunities align with the vision, they strengthen culture. When they are not, they introduce competing priorities and conflicting values. Vision ensures that growth does not come at the cost of identity.

Strong leaders are not defined by how many opportunities they pursue. They are defined by how wisely they choose. Vision gives leaders the courage to walk away from good opportunities to protect a great purpose. It preserves focus. It safeguards resources. It keeps the organization moving in a coherent direction. An organization that filters opportunity through vision grows with intention. An organization that ignores vision grows by accident.

Chapter 6
LAYER THREE: MISSION

An organization's mission defines its current purpose and operational focus. While vision establishes destination, mission defines identity in action. Mission answers the question, "Why do we exist, and what are we here to do right now?" It clarifies how the organization serves, who it serves, and what responsibility it carries in the present.

Mission is not aspirational language. It is not future-oriented dreaming. It is not a description of what the organization hopes to become someday. Mission is the expression of purpose in motion. It defines the work that must be done today to move faithfully toward tomorrow.

A clear mission anchors daily decisions, priorities, and behavior. It establishes what the organization is responsible for delivering and what it is accountable for producing. When the mission is well defined, leaders know what to build, teams know what to execute, and stakeholders know what to expect.

Mission also protects organizational focus. It prevents distraction by narrowing attention to the work that truly matters. Without a mission, organizations become busy but ineffective. Activity increases, but impact diminishes. Energy is spent, but progress stalls.

Within the LCSM10 framework, mission serves as the operational expression of vision. Vision defines destination. Mission defines the direction of movement. Together, they create continuity between future purpose and present action. An organization without a mission lacks clarity. An organization with a mission operates with discipline, alignment, and purpose.

What Mission Is And Is Not

Mission is the clear, present-focused expression of why an organization exists and what it is called to do each day in pursuit of its vision. It defines purpose, not destination. Mission answers the question, "Why do we exist, and what are we responsible for right now?" It provides direction for daily action and focuses leadership, staff, and stakeholders.

Mission is not a slogan. It is not a marketing phrase designed to sound impressive. It is not a list of programs, activities, or departments. It is not a vague statement about good intentions. A mission that lacks clarity becomes decoration rather than direction.

Mission is also not the same as vision. Vision defines where the organization is going. Mission defines what the organization is doing to get there. Vision is future-oriented. Mission is present-oriented. Vision describes the destination. Mission describes responsibility.

A true mission statement is operational, not aspirational. It translates values into action and vision into focus. It defines who the organization serves, what it provides, and how it fulfills its calling. When the mission is clear, priorities are ordered, resources are stewarded wisely, and effort is aligned toward a common purpose.

Mission is not personal ambition. It is not the preference of one leader imposed on others. A shared understanding of purpose unites leadership and staff around a common responsibility. When a mission is properly formed, it creates consistency in decision-making, accountability in execution, and clarity in evaluation.

Mission gives meaning to work. It explains why tasks matter. It justifies discipline and sacrifice. It connects daily effort to lasting impact.

Mission As Organizational Identity →

Mission is the living expression of an organization's identity. It defines who the organization is in practice, not just in principle. While values establish moral character and vision defines future direction, mission reveals how that identity is lived out every day through action, service, and responsibility.

An organization's mission is the clearest statement of what it exists to do and for whom it exists to serve. It clarifies the organization's role in the world and the specific contribution it is called to make. When the mission is clear, people understand not only what the organization believes, but how those beliefs are expressed through daily work. Identity moves from abstract conviction to operational reality.

Mission anchors an organization against distraction and dilution. In seasons of growth, pressure, or opportunity, mission protects focus. It ensures that expansion does not compromise purpose and that success does not replace faithfulness. Leaders use mission to evaluate opportunities, allocate resources, and measure effectiveness. Staff use the mission to understand expectations, align priorities, and take ownership of their work.

A strong mission statement creates organizational coherence. It aligns departments, teams, and individuals around a shared purpose. It prevents fragmentation by giving every role meaning within the organization's larger calling. When the mission is absent or unclear, people operate from personal interpretation rather than shared identity, and unity begins to erode.

Mission is not simply what an organization does. It is who the organization is in action. It is identity expressed through obedience, stewardship, service, and responsibility. When the mission is faithfully lived, the organization becomes recognizable not only by its name but also by its character, conduct, and contributions.

Biblical Models of Mission

Biblical models of mission reveal that God has always defined purpose before assigning action. Throughout Scripture, mission is not a self-generated ambition but a divinely appointed responsibility. God establishes identity, then sends His people to act in accordance with that identity. Mission is always rooted in calling, obedience, and stewardship.

From the beginning, God commissioned humanity with a mission. In Genesis, Adam and Eve were entrusted with the responsibility to steward creation, cultivate the earth, and walk in faithful relationship with God. Their mission was not simply to exist, but to represent God's authority and care within His creation. Identity preceded assignment. Relationship preceded responsibility.

God later called Abraham and gave him a mission that extended far beyond personal blessing. "In you all the families of the earth shall be blessed" (Genesis 12:3). Abraham's mission was not centered on personal prosperity, but on becoming a conduit through which God's purposes would flow to the nations. His obedience shaped generations.

Moses was given a mission to lead God's people out of bondage and into a covenant relationship with the Lord. God did not simply free Israel from Egypt. He commissioned Moses to shepherd, govern, and guide the nation according to God's law. The mission was clear, demanding, and costly, yet it was anchored in God's promise and presence.

Joshua inherited that mission and carried it forward. He was called to lead the people into the Promised Land and establish them as a nation set apart for God. His leadership demonstrates that mission is not merely inherited vision but active obedience. The mission required courage, discipline, and unwavering commitment to God's commands.

Nehemiah provides another powerful model of mission-centered leadership. God placed a burden on his heart for the broken walls of Jerusalem. That burden became his mission. Nehemiah left comfort, faced opposition, endured threats, and organized an entire people around a single purpose: the restoration of God's city and the protection of God's people. His mission was not a political ambition. It was obedience to God's calling.

In the New Testament, Jesus Himself embodied perfect mission. He declared, "For the Son of Man came to seek and to save the lost" (Luke 19:10). His mission defined His ministry, shaped His relationships, governed His priorities, and ultimately led Him to the cross. Every miracle, every teaching, and every sacrifice flowed from His commitment to fulfill the will of the Father.

Before ascending into heaven, Jesus entrusted that mission to His followers. "Go therefore and make disciples of all nations" (Matthew 28:19). The mission of the Church is not self-preservation, popularity, or comfort. It is obedience to Christ's command to proclaim the gospel, disciple believers, and reflect the character of God in the world.

Biblical mission is never vague. It is specific, demanding, and anchored in obedience. It requires sacrifice, courage, and faithfulness. It defines identity in action. When leaders embrace mission as a divine calling rather than a human initiative, organizations move beyond activity and into purpose. Mission becomes the daily expression of obedience to God's will and the living testimony of His work through His people.

Mission And Customer Focus

Mission defines why an organization exists and who it exists to serve. It establishes organizational identity and daily purpose. A mission statement is not a description of internal ambition, nor is it a list of programs or services. It is a declaration of responsibility. It answers the question, "Who are we here for, and what are we called to do for them?"

In organizational leadership, mission functions as the operational expression of purpose. It connects belief to action and vision to behavior. Vision defines destination. Mission defines assignment. Values define conviction. Culture defines practice.

Strategy defines execution. Policy defines protection. When the mission is clear, leadership gains focus, teams gain direction, and decision-making becomes more consistent.

Lucas's (2018) research demonstrated that mission statements directly influence customer satisfaction when they are customer-focused, clear, and consistently reinforced through leadership systems. The study examined the relationships among mission clarity, customer focus, and customer satisfaction and found a statistically significant correlation between customer-focused mission statements and a positive customer experience. In practical terms, organizations that define their purpose around the people they serve build higher trust, stronger loyalty, and greater long-term sustainability.

An inwardly focused mission weakens organizational health. When purpose is centered on internal goals, growth metrics, or institutional preservation, customers become secondary. Over time, service declines, trust erodes, and satisfaction weakens. Organizations may remain busy, but they lose relational connection with the people they exist to serve.

Customer-focused mission reverses that pattern. It places responsibility at the center of leadership. It defines success in terms of impact, care, and stewardship rather than volume, scale, or prestige. It reminds leaders that organizations do not exist for themselves. They exist for others.

For faith-based organizations, customer focus must be understood through a biblical lens. Scripture consistently teaches that leadership is stewardship and service. Jesus defined His own mission in relational terms. He came to seek and save the lost. He came to serve rather than be served. He came to lay down His life for others. His mission was never institutional. It was personal, redemptive, and relational.

In the same way, Christian-led organizations are called to define their purpose in terms of faithful service to the people entrusted to their care. Mission is not about building platforms. It is about building people. It is not about preserving structures. It is about stewarding influence. It is not about protecting comfort. It is about pursuing obedience.

Within the LCSM10 framework, mission serves as the daily expression of organizational purpose. It directs culture. It informs strategy. It anchors policy. It shapes how customers are treated, how problems are solved, how resources are used, and how success is measured.

Lucas (2018) confirmed that when leaders communicate purpose clearly and keep customer focus central, satisfaction increases and trust deepens. Mission becomes more than language. It becomes leadership in action. When the mission is clear, customer focus becomes natural. When the mission is vague, customer focus becomes optional.

Mission is the reason an organization gets up every morning. It is the work that has been entrusted to do. When a mission is defined with clarity, conviction, and customer responsibility, organizations move with purpose, serve with excellence, and lead with integrity.

Mission As Operational Clarity

A mission provides operational clarity by defining what an organization is responsible for doing every day in pursuit of its vision. It translates purpose into action and conviction into practice. Vision answers the question of where the organization is going. Mission answers what the organization is here to do right now. Without a mission, vision remains theoretical. With a mission, vision becomes actionable.

Operational clarity means that people understand their assignment. Leaders know what success looks like. Teams know what matters most. Decisions are evaluated against a clear standard of purpose. When a mission is defined well, it becomes the organizing principle for daily work. It shapes priorities, guides resource allocation, and directs effort toward meaningful outcomes.

Mission is not a slogan or a motivational phrase. It is a governing statement of responsibility. It defines who the organization serves, how it serves them, and why that service matters. It anchors activity in purpose and prevents organizations from becoming distracted by opportunities that do not advance their calling.

When the mission is unclear, organizations become busy but ineffective. Energy is scattered. Programs multiply. Initiatives compete for attention. Leaders react instead of leading. Over time, effort increases while impact declines. People work harder but accomplish less because there is no unifying assignment directing their labor.

Clear mission restores focus. It provides a framework for saying yes and a standard for saying no. It disciplines growth. It protects culture. It keeps the organization oriented toward service rather than self-preservation. It ensures that every role, department, and leader understands how their work contributes to the whole.

Within the LCSM10 framework, mission functions as the operational backbone of alignment. It connects values to culture, vision to strategy, and leadership language to daily behavior. It ensures that organizational purpose is not merely spoken, but lived.

Mission is not an abstract idea. It is the daily work of leadership. It is the assignment entrusted to the organization. When the mission is clear, organizations move with direction, serve with intention, and operate with disciplined purpose.

Why Mission Gets Ignored

Mission is often ignored, not because leaders reject its importance, but because urgency crowds out purpose. Daily demands, operational pressure, financial concerns, staffing challenges, and crisis management slowly replace intentional leadership. Over time, organizations become reactive rather than proactive. They respond to what is loudest rather than what is most important. When this happens, the mission becomes a framed statement on a wall rather than a governing standard for decision-making.

Another reason the mission is neglected is that many organizations confuse activity with impact. Busyness creates the illusion of productivity. Programs multiply. Meetings increase. Calendars fill. Yet without a clearly defined mission guiding those activities, effort becomes scattered. People work hard, but their work is not always aligned. Energy is expended without advancing the organization toward its purpose. When the mission is unclear, success is measured by motion instead of progress.

Mission also gets ignored when leadership changes or grows without intentional alignment. New leaders bring new ideas. New staff bring new expectations. New opportunities introduce new directions. If the mission is not continually taught, reinforced, and protected, it slowly loses authority. Decisions begin to reflect personal preferences rather than organizational purpose. Over time, the organization drifts from
its original calling.

Fear also plays a role. A clear mission requires discipline. It requires saying no to good opportunities that do not serve the organization's purpose. It requires closing programs that no longer align with the organization's goals. It requires confronting misaligned behavior. Many leaders avoid this discomfort by keeping the mission vague. A vague mission makes accountability difficult and preserves short-term harmony at the cost of long-term effectiveness.

Finally, the mission is ignored when it is written in inspirational language rather than as an operational responsibility. If a mission statement is poetic but impractical, people do not know how to apply it. If it is broad and generic, it does not guide real decisions. When a mission lacks clarity, it loses authority. When it lacks relevance, it loses influence.

Organizations do not intentionally abandon their mission. They abandon it gradually. Drift begins quietly. Distraction grows subtly. Over time, purpose fades into background noise. The result is an organization that is busy, stressed, and well-intentioned, yet no longer clearly focused on its purpose.

Recovering a mission requires leadership discipline. It requires clarity, consistency, and courage. It requires returning to first principles and rebuilding alignment from the foundation up. When the mission is restored to its proper place, organizations regain focus, unity, and direction.

How Mission Drives Decision-Making →

Mission functions as the operating compass of an organization. It defines why the organization exists and what it is responsible for accomplishing in the present. When a mission is clearly articulated and consistently applied, it becomes the primary filter through which every major decision is evaluated. It shapes priorities, governs resource allocation, directs leadership focus, and establishes the standard by which success is measured.

A clearly defined mission brings discipline to leadership. It prevents reactionary decision-making driven by pressure, emotion, or trend. Instead of asking, "Is this a good opportunity?" leaders can ask, "Does this advance our mission?" This distinction protects the organization from distraction. Many opportunities appear attractive on the surface, but if they do not directly support the organization's purpose, they dilute focus and weaken impact. Mission provides the clarity to say no to what is merely good and to pursue what is essential.

Mission also creates consistency across leadership levels. When the mission is understood and owned by executives, managers, and frontline leaders alike, decisions become aligned. Teams begin to operate with a shared understanding of what matters most. This reduces internal conflict, minimizes confusion, and strengthens trust. When people know the mission, they can make sound decisions even when leadership is not present, because they understand the framework that governs judgment.

From an operational perspective, mission translates purpose into action. It informs how programs are designed, how staff are trained, how customers are served, and how performance is evaluated. Hiring decisions are shaped by mission fit. Mission priorities shape budget decisions. Strategic planning is shaped by mission direction. Over time, the mission becomes embedded in the organization's culture, not as a slogan but as a living standard.

Mission also provides stability during seasons of change. Markets shift. Technology evolves. Leadership transitions occur. Economic conditions fluctuate. In each of these moments, organizations anchored in mission can adapt without losing their identity. The methods may change, but the purpose remains constant. This continuity builds resilience and preserves organizational integrity.

Ultimately, a mission gives meaning to leadership responsibility. It clarifies what leaders are accountable for stewarding. It defines what must be protected. It establishes what must be pursued. When the mission is honored, decisions gain coherence, strategy gains direction, and the organization gains focus.

When the mission is ignored, decisions become fragmented, priorities compete, and leadership becomes reactive. When the mission is central, leadership becomes intentional, aligned, and effective.

Mission As Daily Direction

Mission is the daily expression of an organization's purpose. It translates long-term vision into present responsibility and turns values into action. While vision defines where the organization is going, mission defines what the organization is doing right now to move toward that destination. It gives practical direction to leadership, staff, and teams by clarifying what matters most in everyday operations.

A clear mission provides focus amid constant activity. Organizations are filled with competing demands, urgent requests, and unexpected challenges. Without a defined mission, leaders and teams are forced to rely on instinct, pressure, or habit to determine priorities. This leads to reactive behavior and fragmented effort. A strong mission establishes a shared understanding of purpose that guides daily decisions, workflows, and problem-solving.

Mission also shapes how work is performed. It defines not only what the organization does, but how it does it. It influences the tone of leadership, the standard of service, and the way people are treated. When the mission is clear, employees understand how their roles contribute to something larger than their job description. This creates ownership, motivation, and accountability.

In daily practice, mission becomes the framework for evaluating tasks and commitments. Leaders can ask whether a meeting, program, or initiative directly supports the organization's purpose. Teams can assess whether their time and energy are being invested in work that advances the mission or simply fills the calendar. This discipline protects the organization from drift and helps maintain alignment between intention and execution.

Mission also provides stability in moments of pressure. When difficult decisions must be made, the mission serves as the reference point. It clarifies what must be preserved, what can be adjusted, and what should be discontinued. This prevents short-term convenience from undermining long-term purpose and keeps leadership grounded in responsibility rather than reaction.

Chapter 7
LAYER INTEGRATION

Eliminate Fragmentation

Values, vision, and mission are not independent concepts. They function as an integrated leadership system that creates alignment, clarity, and organizational coherence. When properly constructed and consistently applied, they eliminate fragmentation by ensuring that belief, direction, and action move together in a unified framework.

Values define what the organization stands for. They establish the moral and ethical foundation that governs behavior, decision-making, and leadership conduct. Values answer the question of what is right, what is important, and what will be defended regardless of cost or convenience. They shape culture, determine standards, and establish the boundaries of acceptable behavior. Without clearly defined values, organizations drift into inconsistency, personality-driven leadership, and situational ethics.

Vision defines where the organization is going. It establishes a future destination that gives long-term direction and meaning to present effort. Vision answers the question of what the organization is becoming and what future it is pursuing. It provides a shared horizon that unifies leadership, aligns strategy, and anchors long-range planning. Vision prevents short-term pressure from replacing long-term purpose and protects the organization from reactive decision-making.

Mission defines what the organization is doing right now to move toward its vision. It translates values into action and vision into daily responsibility. A mission answers the question of why the organization exists and what it is accountable for accomplishing in the present. It gives operational focus, guides daily priorities, and provides clarity for staff, teams, and stakeholders.

When these three elements function together, alignment is created across every layer of leadership and operation. Values shape vision by defining the kind of future worth pursuing. Vision gives direction to the mission by establishing a destination that daily work must support. Mission gives expression to values and vision through disciplined execution.

Fragmentation occurs when these elements are disconnected. Values without vision create conviction without direction. Vision without mission creates inspiration without execution. Mission without values creates activity without integrity. Vision without values becomes ambition. Mission without vision becomes busyness. Values without mission become ideology.

An aligned organization does not rely on personality, pressure, or momentum to move forward. It is governed by convictions, directed by purpose, and guided by discipline. Values establish the standard. Vision establishes the destination. Mission establishes the path.

When values, vision, and mission are clearly defined and faithfully practiced, leadership gains credibility, culture gains stability, strategy gains focus, and decisions gain consistency. Fragmentation is replaced with alignment. Confusion is replaced with clarity. Drift is replaced with direction.

This integration is the foundation of healthy leadership and sustainable organizational growth.

Prepare Leaders For Culture Work

Culture is not created by accident. It is formed by leadership behavior, reinforced by organizational systems, and sustained through consistent accountability. Leaders do not inherit a healthy culture. They build it, protect it, and steward it over time. Preparing leaders for culture work is essential because culture reflects what leadership truly values, not merely what leadership claims.

Culture is the lived expression of values, vision, and mission. It is what people experience when policies are tested, pressure is applied, and decisions must be made quickly. It reveals what is tolerated, what is rewarded, and what is corrected. Leaders shape culture through what they model, what they permit, and what they confront. Every decision, conversation, and response becomes a cultural signal.

Leaders must understand that cultural work is not motivational. It is structural. It requires intentional systems, clear standards, disciplined communication, and consistent enforcement. A healthy culture does not emerge from good intentions. It emerges from clearly defined, faithfully applied governing principles.

Preparing leaders for culture work means training them to recognize cultural drift before it becomes organizational decay. It means equipping them to identify misalignment between stated values and practiced behavior. It means giving them the tools to correct dysfunction with courage, clarity, and conviction. It also means teaching leaders to build environments where excellence is expected, integrity is protected, accountability is normal, and trust is earned.

Culture work is slow, deliberate, and demanding. It requires patience without compromise and compassion without weakness. Leaders must be prepared to lead through resistance, discomfort, and change. They must be willing to confront behavior that undermines the organization's values, even when that behavior comes from high performers or influential personalities.

A healthy culture does not depend on charisma. It depends on consistency. It does not depend on emotion. It depends on the discipline. It does not depend on popularity. It depends on the principle. Organizations rise or fall on culture. Leaders either steward it intentionally or inherit its consequences. Preparing leaders for culture work is preparing them for their most enduring responsibility: shaping the environment in which people serve, grow, and build together.

Why Fragmented Leadership Fails →

Fragmented leadership fails because organizations cannot move in a unified direction when authority is divided, priorities are unclear, and accountability is inconsistent. When leaders operate from disconnected values, competing visions, or personal agendas, the organization loses coherence. Decisions become reactive instead of strategic. Culture becomes unstable. Trust erodes. Over time, fragmentation produces confusion, inefficiency, and drift.

Leadership fragmentation occurs when values are assumed rather than defined, when vision is interpreted rather than shared, and when mission is treated as optional rather than governing. In these conditions, departments pursue their own objectives, managers create independent standards, and teams begin operating in silos. The organization may remain busy, but it is no longer aligned. Activity increases while effectiveness declines.

Fragmented leadership also creates conflicting authority. When multiple leaders establish competing expectations, staff are forced to choose whose direction to follow. This produces uncertainty, political behavior, and decision paralysis. People stop asking what is right for the organization and start asking what will keep them out of trouble. Innovation slows. Initiative declines. Accountability weakens.

From a biblical perspective, fragmentation undermines stewardship. Scripture consistently emphasizes unity, order, and shared purpose among leaders. When leadership lacks agreement, the people suffer. Proverbs teaches that where there is no wise direction, the people fall. Unity among leaders is not optional. It is foundational to effective governance and faithful service.

Fragmentation also destroys long-term sustainability. Organizations cannot scale, grow, or endure when leadership is divided. Systems break down. Policies are ignored. Standards erode. Culture becomes inconsistent and unpredictable. Eventually, the organization becomes personality-driven rather than principle-governed, making it vulnerable to instability whenever leadership changes.

Effective leadership requires alignment across values, vision, and mission. Leaders must operate from a shared framework, a common language, and a unified direction. Authority must be clear. Expectations must be consistent. Accountability must be enforced. When leadership is aligned, organizations move with strength, clarity, and resilience.

Fragmented leadership fails because it replaces unity with competition, clarity with confusion, and purpose with politics. Aligned leadership builds trust, stability, and momentum. Organizations that endure are not led by isolated leaders, but by unified leadership teams anchored in shared conviction and shared direction.

Statement Consistency

Statement consistency is the discipline of ensuring that values, vision, mission, culture, strategy, and policy operate as a single, unified system rather than as disconnected documents. An organization does not become aligned because it has statements. It becomes aligned when those statements reinforce one another, communicate the same direction, and govern behavior consistently across every level of leadership.

When statements are inconsistent, organizations experience internal friction. Leaders communicate mixed priorities. Departments pursue competing objectives. Policies contradict stated values. Culture drifts away from vision. Over time, people stop trusting the statements because they no longer reflect reality. Statements become wall décor rather than governing standards.

Consistency begins with values. Values define the moral and ethical foundation of leadership. Vision builds on those values by establishing the future direction the organization is pursuing. Mission then translates vision into present-day purpose and operational focus. Culture reflects how values, vision, and mission are lived daily. Strategy determines how the mission is executed. Policy protects all of them through formal structure and accountability. When any layer breaks alignment, the entire framework weakens.

Statement consistency also protects decision-making. Leaders must be able to evaluate opportunities, initiatives, and investments through the same lens. When values say one thing, vision suggests another, and mission directs something else, leadership loses credibility. Staff are left guessing what truly matters. Consistency restores confidence by establishing a clear, reliable standard for action.

From a leadership perspective, consistency establishes authority. People follow leaders they trust. Trust is built when words and actions match. When organizational statements remain stable, coherent, and reinforced through leadership behavior, they become a source of unity and direction. When they change frequently, contradict one another, or are ignored, they become irrelevant.

Statement consistency is not achieved through editing alone. It requires disciplined governance, leadership accountability, and continual reinforcement. Leaders must model the statements, teach them, apply them, and protect them. Every major decision should be traceable to them. Every policy should support them. Every strategy should advance them.

Organizations that endure are not guided by disconnected ideas, but by integrated convictions. When values, vision, mission, culture, strategy, and policy speak with one voice, leadership gains clarity, people gain confidence, and the organization gains strength.

Organizational Coherence

Organizational coherence is the condition in which every part of the organization moves in the same direction, under the same convictions, toward the same destination. It exists when leadership, culture, strategy, and policy operate in harmony rather than in competition. Coherence is not created by structure alone. It is created by alignment of belief, direction, purpose, and action.

An organization is coherent when its values shape behavior, its vision defines direction, its mission governs daily focus, its culture reflects those convictions in practice, its strategy advances the mission, and its policies protect the entire framework. When these elements function together, leadership becomes stable, decision-making becomes consistent, and the organization gains long-term strength.

Coherence eliminates internal friction. Departments no longer compete for influence. Leaders no longer send mixed signals. Staff no longer operate under conflicting priorities. When coherence is present, people understand not only what the organization does, but why it exists, where it is going, and how they contribute to that future. Unity replaces confusion. Purpose replaces activity.

Incoherence, by contrast, creates fragmentation. Vision becomes disconnected from operations. Values become disconnected from behavior. Policies become disconnected from conviction. Strategy becomes disconnected from mission. Over time, people stop trusting leadership direction because it no longer reflects lived reality. Momentum slows. Morale weakens. Drift sets in.

Organizational coherence is built intentionally. It requires disciplined leadership, clear communication, and structural integrity. Leaders must govern through their statements, not merely publish them. They must evaluate decisions through them, measure performance against them, and hold teams accountable to them. Coherence is sustained through consistency.

A coherent organization does not rely on personality, charisma, or momentum. It relies on alignment. It moves forward with stability because every part supports the whole. When coherence is established, leadership gains authority, teams gain confidence, and the organization gains the capacity to grow without losing its identity.

Organizations that endure are not simply well-managed. They are well aligned.

Leadership Credibility

Leadership credibility is the foundation of organizational trust, authority, and long-term influence. It is not granted by title, position, or seniority. It is earned through consistent alignment between what leaders say, what they decide, and how they live. When leaders govern with integrity and clarity, people follow with confidence. When leaders drift from their stated convictions, credibility erodes, and authority weakens.

Credibility is built when values are practiced, not merely published. It is strengthened when vision guides decisions rather than when decisions are adjusted for convenience. It is reinforced when mission governs daily priorities instead of being ignored under pressure. Leaders who operate with consistency create stability. Leaders who compromise direction for short-term gain create confusion and distrust.

Organizations watch leadership behavior more closely than leadership language. Teams evaluate credibility by observing how leaders respond to conflict, handle failure, treat people, and steward resources. When values are enforced only when it is easy, credibility disappears. When convictions are upheld even when it is costly, credibility grows.

Credible leadership produces confidence across the organization. Staff feel secure in decision-making because standards are clear. Teams take ownership because direction is stable. Stakeholders develop trust because promises are kept. Customers experience reliability because culture reflects conviction. Over time, credibility becomes the organization's reputation.

Without credibility, leadership authority becomes positional rather than moral. Compliance replaces commitment. Silence replaces honesty. Politics replaces purpose. Momentum slows because people no longer believe direction is real or enduring.

Leadership credibility is preserved through discipline. Leaders must submit themselves to the same standards they require of others. They must evaluate their decisions through the lens of their values, vision, and mission. They must communicate clearly, act consistently, and correct misalignment quickly. Credibility is not a personality trait. It is a leadership responsibility.

Organizations rise or fall on the credibility of their leaders. When leadership is trusted, organizations move forward with unity and strength. When leadership is doubted, even the best strategy cannot overcome internal fracture.

What Misalignment Looks Like

Organizational misalignment occurs when values, vision, and mission no longer operate as a unified framework. It is the slow separation between what leaders say, what the organization claims, and what people experience in daily practice. Misalignment rarely happens all at once. It develops gradually through small compromises, inconsistent decisions, and unaddressed drift.

Misalignment is visible when stated values are ignored under pressure. Leaders may affirm integrity but tolerate unethical shortcuts to meet financial targets. They may speak of accountability but avoid hard conversations. They may claim excellence while accepting mediocrity. Over time, people learn that values are optional rather than governing.

Misalignment occurs when vision is treated as decoration rather than direction. Vision statements may hang on walls and appear on websites, but they no longer guide budgeting, hiring, program development, or long-term planning. Leaders begin to chase attractive opportunities that pull the organization away from its intended destination. Growth becomes reactive rather than intentional.

Misalignment is evident when the mission loses operational authority. Teams become busy but unfocused. Departments pursue their own priorities. Projects multiply without coordination. Leaders measure activity instead of impact. The organization works harder but moves less.

Misalignment also shows itself in culture. When values, vision, and mission are fragmented, culture becomes unstable. Staff experience confusion about expectations. Conflict increases because standards are unclear. Morale declines because effort feels disconnected from purpose. Turnover rises because people no longer understand what the organization stands for or where it is going.

Externally, misalignment damages reputation. Customers receive inconsistent experiences. Partners struggle to understand priorities. Stakeholders lose confidence in leadership. Trust weakens because the organization no longer behaves in a predictable, principled way.

Misalignment is not merely an operational problem. It is a leadership failure. It reflects the absence of disciplined governance and the neglect of organizational architecture. When alignment is not intentionally maintained, fragmentation becomes inevitable.

Healthy organizations operate with coherence. Values govern behavior. Vision directs the future. Mission drives daily action. When these elements function together, leadership is strong, culture is stable, and direction is clear.

The Cost of Inconsistency

Inconsistency is one of the most damaging forces in leadership and organizational life. It erodes trust, weakens authority, confuses culture, and undermines long-term stability. While inconsistency may appear minor in isolated decisions, its cumulative effect reshapes an organization's identity and direction.

Inconsistent leadership creates uncertainty. When leaders apply values selectively, enforce standards unevenly, or change direction without explanation, people no longer know what to expect. Predictability is replaced with hesitation. Confidence is replaced with caution. Teams begin to operate defensively rather than decisively, unsure whether today's expectations will still matter tomorrow.

Inconsistency also destroys credibility. Leaders may speak about integrity, accountability, excellence, or stewardship, but when those principles are not consistently demonstrated, words lose their authority. People learn to distinguish between what leadership says and what leadership actually does. Over time, statements become background noise rather than governing standards.

Culture suffers most under inconsistency. Culture is built through repeated behavior, not written language. When leadership behavior changes based on pressure, convenience, or emotion, culture becomes unstable. Standards fluctuate. Expectations blur. What was once unacceptable becomes tolerated. What was once required becomes optional.

Operationally, inconsistency leads to inefficiency. Teams spend time navigating unclear priorities, revisiting decisions, and correcting preventable mistakes. Resources are wasted on misaligned initiatives. Strategy becomes reactive rather than intentional. Momentum slows as energy is spent managing confusion rather than advancing purpose.

Relationally, inconsistency breeds resentment. High-performing individuals become discouraged when effort is not rewarded fairly. Others become complacent when underperformance is tolerated. Unity fractures as people perceive favoritism, unpredictability, or hidden standards.

Externally, inconsistency damages reputation. Customers experience uneven service. Partners lose confidence. Stakeholders question leadership stability. Trust weakens when the organization cannot be relied upon to fulfill its stated commitments.

Inconsistency is not a personality flaw. It is a governance failure. It reflects the absence of a disciplined leadership architecture. Without clear values, an anchored vision, and an operational mission, leaders are left making decisions under pressure rather than principle.

Sustainable organizations are built on consistency. Consistency of conviction. Consistency of direction. Consistency of behavior. When leadership is consistent, culture stabilizes, trust grows, and the organization gains the strength required for long-term impact.

Alignment Under Pressure

Alignment is easy when conditions are favorable. It is tested when pressure rises. Every organization eventually encounters moments where speed, money, fear, competition, conflict, or fatigue tempt leaders to compromise standards for short-term relief. Those moments reveal whether alignment is real or merely aspirational.

Pressure exposes the difference between written statements and governing convictions. When revenue declines, values are tested. When conflict escalates, unity is tested. When opportunity appears attractive but misaligned, vision is tested. When shortcuts promise faster results, integrity is tested. Under pressure, leaders discover whether their values function as anchors or decorations.

Organizations that lack alignment respond to pressure reactively. Decisions become situational. Standards bend. Exceptions multiply. What was once non-negotiable becomes negotiable. Over time, compromise becomes normalized, and drift becomes institutionalized.

Aligned organizations respond to pressure with discipline. Leaders return to first principles. Values define boundaries. Vision clarifies direction. Mission reinforces focus. Strategy remains anchored. Pressure becomes a refining force rather than a destabilizing one.

Alignment under pressure creates stability. Teams know what matters. Decisions follow a known framework. Authority is exercised consistently. Accountability remains intact. Even difficult choices are understood because they follow clearly established convictions.

Pressure also reveals leadership maturity. Immature leadership avoids tension by lowering standards. Mature leadership carries tension by upholding standards. The strength of leadership is not measured by how well it performs in calm seasons but by how faithfully it governs in difficult ones.

Scripture consistently affirms this principle. Testing reveals foundation. Storms reveal structure. Fire reveals purity. In the same way, pressure reveals alignment.

Organizations that endure do not survive solely on adaptability. They survive by conviction. Alignment is what allows leaders to stand firm when compromise would be easier, when fear would be safer, and when convenience would be more comfortable.

Alignment under pressure is not rigidity. It is fidelity. It is leadership that refuses to trade long-term integrity for short-term relief. It is governance that remains faithful when circumstances demand sacrifice. This is where leadership earns trust, where culture is protected, and where organizations either drift or endure.

PART III

CULTURE, STRATEGY, AND POLICY

Turning Belief Into Behavior

This section marks the transition from conviction to execution. Values, vision, and mission establish identity and direction. Culture, strategy, and policy determine whether that direction is actually followed. This is where leadership moves from intention to implementation, from belief to behavior, and from statements to systems.

Many organizations possess strong convictions but lack consistent execution. They know what they believe, but they struggle to translate belief into daily conduct. Culture, strategy, and policy exist to close that gap. They operationalize leadership. They turn principles into patterns. They convert ideals into habits.

Culture is the lived environment created by repeated behavior. It is what people experience when no one is watching. It reflects what leadership tolerates, rewards, and corrects. Strategy is the disciplined plan that directs resources, effort, and priorities toward the vision. Policy is the governing structure that protects values, guides decisions, and enforces accountability.

Together, these three layers form the operational backbone of the organization. They determine how people are treated, how decisions are made, how conflicts are resolved, how risks are managed, and how success is measured. They provide the structure that allows an organization to grow without losing its identity.

This is where leadership becomes visible. This is where credibility is tested. This is where alignment either holds or collapses.

Belief alone does not build organizations. Behavior does. And behavior is shaped by culture, directed by strategy, and protected by policy. Part III is where leadership becomes real.

Chapter 8: Culture

The Lived Expression of Leadership

Show How Beliefs Become Behavior →

Beliefs only shape an organization when they are translated into daily conduct. Until convictions are expressed through consistent action, they remain ideas rather than leadership. The movement from belief to behavior is the defining work of culture, strategy, and policy. These three layers determine whether values, vision, and mission remain theoretical or become operational.

Beliefs become behavior through repetition, reinforcement, and accountability. When leaders consistently model their convictions, reward alignment, and correct deviation, values move from paper into practice. Culture forms as people observe what is honored, what is ignored, and what is enforced. Strategy channels belief into disciplined action by directing time, resources, and effort toward the organization's stated future. Policy formalizes belief into governing standards that protect integrity, guide decisions, and provide clarity under pressure.

Organizations do not drift toward excellence. They drift toward what they tolerate. Behavior follows the path of least resistance unless leadership intentionally builds systems that reinforce its beliefs. When values are clear, but culture is weak, belief erodes. When vision is strong but strategy is unfocused, effort is wasted. When the mission is compelling, but policy is absent, accountability disappears.

Beliefs become behavior when leaders design environments that make the right actions normal, expected, and measurable. Over time, those actions become habits. Those habits become culture. That culture becomes the organization's identity.

This is the work of leadership. Not merely to declare what is right, but to build structures that make what is right sustainable.

What Culture Really Is

Culture is the lived expression of what an organization truly believes. It is not what is written in handbooks, posted on walls, or declared from platforms. Culture is what people experience when they walk into the building, sit in meetings, interact with leadership, and observe how decisions are made. It is the environment created by repeated behavior over time.

Culture is shaped by what leaders model, reward, tolerate, and correct. Every organization has a culture, whether it is intentional or accidental. When leaders do not define culture, it will define itself through habit, personality, pressure, and convenience. Over time, those patterns become the organization's identity.

Culture is not morale. It is not personality. It is not the atmosphere. It is not branding. Culture is the operational expression of values in daily life. It is how people speak to one another, how conflict is handled, how excellence is pursued, how accountability is enforced, and how people are treated under pressure.

Culture answers the question, "How do we actually operate here?" It reveals whether stated beliefs are real or decorative. If values say integrity, but leaders tolerate dishonesty, the culture is dishonesty. If values say excellence, but mediocrity is accepted, the culture is one of complacency. If values say accountability, but correction never happens, the culture is avoidance.

Culture is built through consistency. When leadership behavior aligns with stated values, trust grows. When leadership behavior contradicts stated values, credibility collapses. Over time, people stop listening to what leaders say and begin watching what leaders do.

Culture is not created solely by intention. It is created by discipline. It is maintained by leadership courage. It is protected by policy. It is strengthened by accountability. It is sustained by example.

An organization will never rise above its culture. It will only rise as high as the standards it enforces and the convictions it lives by.

How Culture Is Formed →

Culture is formed through repetition. It is the accumulation of daily decisions, leadership behavior, and organizational responses over time. It develops not from what leaders intend, but from what leaders consistently do. Every choice, every correction, every reward, and every silence contributes to shaping the environment people experience.

Culture begins with leadership. What leaders model becomes permission. What leaders celebrate becomes aspiration. What leaders tolerate becomes standard. What leaders correct becomes expectation. Over time, these signals teach people what truly matters and how they are expected to behave.

Culture is formed through systems. Hiring practices, training methods, evaluation standards, promotion criteria, compensation structures, and discipline processes all reinforce behavioral norms. If systems reward speed over integrity, the culture becomes reckless. If systems reward results without accountability, the culture becomes corrupt. If systems reward faithfulness, excellence, and humility, the culture becomes disciplined and principled.

Culture is formed through communication. What is emphasized in meetings, what is repeated in training, what is discussed in leadership conversations, and what is addressed publicly shapes collective understanding. Silence also communicates. When issues are ignored, people assume they are acceptable. When excellence is never acknowledged, people assume it is unnecessary.

Culture is formed under pressure. When crises arise, people watch leadership closely. How leaders respond to conflict, failure, financial stress, or public scrutiny reveals the organization's true convictions. Pressure exposes whether values are real or merely theoretical.

Culture is formed through consistency. Sporadic enforcement creates confusion. Inconsistent discipline creates cynicism. Selective accountability creates distrust. When expectations are applied equally and upheld faithfully, culture stabilizes.

Culture is not built in a single event. It is built through thousands of small decisions made with discipline over time. It is reinforced every day by what is rewarded, corrected, and ignored. Eventually, those patterns become identity.

An organization does not choose whether it will have a culture. It chooses whether that culture will be intentional or accidental.

Leadership As Culture Architect

Leadership is the primary architect of organizational culture. Culture does not emerge randomly. It is intentionally or unintentionally designed by those who carry authority, set direction, and establish standards. Every organization is shaped by its leadership's priorities, convictions, and behaviors. Over time, these elements form the environment in which people think, work, decide, and relate.

Leaders design culture through example. What leaders practice becomes permission for others. What leaders model becomes expectation. What leaders ignore becomes acceptable. What leaders correct becomes standard. People do not follow written statements nearly as closely as they follow lived behavior. The daily conduct of leadership becomes the blueprint for the organization's culture.

Leaders design culture through decisions. How leaders allocate resources, whom they promote, what they reward, and what they discipline sends clear messages about what matters most. When decisions consistently align with stated values, culture becomes stable and trustworthy. When decisions contradict stated values, culture becomes cynical and fragmented.

Leaders design culture through structure. Reporting lines, authority levels, accountability systems, and communication channels all shape behavior. Structure either reinforces integrity and clarity or enables confusion and dysfunction. A well-designed structure protects values and promotes healthy patterns of behavior across the organization.

Leaders design culture through enforcement. Standards that are not enforced become suggestions. Policies that are not applied consistently become meaningless. Selective accountability becomes unjust. Faithful enforcement establishes safety, trust, and stability. It also protects the organization from drift and decay.

Leaders design culture through presence. Where leaders spend their time, what they pay attention to, and how they engage with people communicate priorities more loudly than any formal document. Presence signals importance. Absence signals indifference.

Culture is never neutral. It is always forming. Leaders are either shaping it intentionally or allowing it to be shaped by pressure, personalities, and circumstance. Organizations do not rise or fall by accident. They rise or fall according to the culture that leadership builds.

Leadership is not only responsible for results. Leadership is responsible for the environment that produces those results. The culture leaders design today determines the behavior the organization will exhibit tomorrow.

What Gets Rewarded And Tolerated →

Organizational culture is formed most powerfully by what leadership rewards and tolerates. Over time, these two forces define the true operating values of an organization, regardless of what is written in statements, policies, or handbooks. People quickly learn what is celebrated, what is ignored, and what is excused, and they adjust their behavior accordingly.

Reward communicates priority. When leaders publicly recognize certain behaviors, promote individuals who model specific attitudes, or provide incentives tied to particular outcomes, they are declaring what matters most. Employees and team members naturally move toward what affirms, advances, and provides security. If integrity is praised, people pursue integrity. If productivity is rewarded without regard for character, people pursue results at any cost. If loyalty is valued over truth, people protect relationships rather than confront problems.

Tolerance communicates permission. When leaders overlook unethical conduct, excuse repeated failures, ignore disrespectful behavior, or avoid addressing dysfunction, they silently authorize those patterns to continue. Tolerated behavior becomes accepted behavior. Accepted behavior becomes normalized behavior. Normalized behavior becomes culture. Over time, what once would have been unthinkable becomes routine.

Culture is not shaped by what leaders say they believe. It is shaped by what leaders consistently reward and consistently tolerate. If leaders claim to value accountability but tolerate irresponsibility, accountability disappears. If leaders claim to value excellence but reward speed over quality, mediocrity becomes the standard. If leaders claim to value unity but tolerate gossip and division, trust erodes.

Healthy organizations establish alignment between belief, behavior, and consequence. When values are consistently reinforced through reward and protected through correction, culture becomes stable and trustworthy. People know where boundaries are. They understand expectations. They feel secure in the standards that govern behavior.

Leaders must regularly examine their own patterns of response. Every promotion, every bonus, every public compliment, and every unaddressed issue sends a message. Over time, those messages form the organization's invisible rulebook.

Culture is built one decision at a time. It is reinforced one response at a time. It is protected one correction at a time. What leaders reward and what leaders tolerate will ultimately determine who the organization becomes.

Culture Under Pressure

Organizational culture is most clearly revealed under pressure. When resources are tight, deadlines are urgent, conflict is present, or uncertainty is high, the true value of leadership emerges. Pressure does not create culture. It exposes it. In moments of stress, people revert to what is most deeply ingrained, not what is most recently taught.

When pressure increases, systems weaken, and habits take over. Policies may be ignored. Procedures may be bypassed. Formal language may be abandoned. What remains is the organization's real culture, the beliefs that leaders actually trust, the behaviors they instinctively defend, and the standards they are willing to sacrifice to survive.

In healthy organizations, pressure strengthens alignment. Leaders return to values. Decisions become slower, more deliberate, and more principled. Communication becomes clearer. Accountability becomes more visible. The organization closes ranks around its convictions and protects its integrity, even when doing so is costly.

In unhealthy organizations, pressure accelerates drift. Ethics becomes negotiable. Boundaries blur. Short-term survival replaces long-term stewardship. Leaders justify compromise as a necessity.

Over time, repeated compromise reshapes the organization into something it never intended to become.

Pressure tests whether values are truly governing standards or merely decorative language. If values disappear when circumstances become difficult, they were never values. They were preferences. True values remain intact when the cost of obedience is high.

Scripture consistently shows that testing reveals the condition of the heart. In the same way, organizational pressure reveals the condition of leadership. It shows whether leaders are anchored in conviction or driven by fear. It shows whether integrity is foundational or expendable. It shows whether people are being stewarded or used.

Organizations that prepare for pressure build resilience into their culture. They train leaders to decide slowly. They establish clear boundaries before a crisis arrives. They define non-negotiables in advance. They commit to truth even when it threatens comfort.

Pressure will come. Markets will change. Crises will arise. Conflict will surface. When it does, culture will speak louder than policy, strategy, and vision statements.

The question is not whether pressure will test the organization. The question is whether the culture will hold.

Toxic Versus Healthy Cultures

Every organization has a culture. The difference is not whether culture exists, but whether it is healthy or toxic. Culture is the invisible system of beliefs, behaviors, expectations, and norms that governs how people actually work, relate, decide, and lead. It is not what is written on the wall. It is what is practiced in the hallway.

A healthy culture is built on clarity, trust, accountability, and shared purpose. People understand what the organization stands for, what is expected of them, and how decisions are made. Leadership is consistent. Standards are enforced fairly. Communication is direct and respectful. Success is celebrated without arrogance, and failure is addressed without shame. People feel safe to speak, to grow, and to take responsibility. In a healthy culture, values are lived, not merely stated.

A toxic culture is built on fear, confusion, inconsistency, and self-protection. Expectations change without explanation. Standards are applied selectively. Leaders say one thing and reward another. Political behavior replaces principled leadership. People learn quickly what to avoid, whom to appease, and when to stay silent. Over time, survival replaces service, and compliance replaces commitment.

Toxic cultures do not usually begin with bad intentions. They develop when leaders fail to define values, tolerate poor behavior, avoid hard conversations, or compromise under pressure. Small lapses become patterns. Patterns become norms. Norms become identity. Eventually, the organization no longer remembers what it was meant to be.

Healthy cultures require intentional leadership. They require clarity of values, discipline in adhering to standards, and courage to confront misalignment. Leaders must model what they expect. They must reward what they want repeated. They must correct what threatens integrity. Culture does not improve through slogans. It improves over time through consistent leadership behavior.

The long-term cost of a toxic culture is always greater than the short-term cost of correction. Toxic cultures drive away strong leaders, discourage initiative, weaken morale, and damage trust. Healthy cultures attract talent, strengthen commitment, increase performance, and build resilience.

Organizations do not rise or fall primarily because of strategy, resources, or opportunity. They rise or fall because of culture. When culture is healthy, growth is sustainable. When culture is toxic, success is temporary.

Culture is the soil in which every vision grows, and every mission operates. If the soil is poisoned, nothing flourishes for long.

Why Culture Eats Strategy

Strategy defines what an organization plans to do. Culture determines what actually happens. No matter how well designed a strategy may be, it will always be filtered through the beliefs, habits, incentives, and behaviors of the people responsible for carrying it out. If culture is weak, confused, or misaligned, even the best strategy will fail in execution.

Strategy lives on paper. Culture lives in people. Strategy outlines direction, goals, and methods. Culture governs how decisions are made, how problems are solved, how authority is exercised, and how responsibility is carried. When the two are aligned, momentum is created. When they are misaligned, resistance forms, often quietly and persistently.

A strong strategy requires discipline, accountability, and trust to succeed. A toxic or unclear culture undermines each of these. If people are afraid to speak honestly, problems go unreported. If favoritism is tolerated, accountability disappears. If standards are inconsistent, execution becomes uneven. Over time, people stop believing in the strategy, not because it is flawed, but because the environment makes faithful execution impossible.

Culture shapes how people respond to pressure. When strategy demands sacrifice, culture determines whether people rally or retreat. When strategy requires change, culture determines whether people adapt or resist. When strategy requires long-term thinking, culture determines whether leaders remain patient or chase short-term comfort.

Many organizations fail not because they lack intelligence or opportunity, but because their culture quietly sabotages their plans. Leaders approve strategies that look impressive, but they do not build the cultural systems required to support them. As a result, the organization becomes skilled at planning and weak at execution.

A healthy culture gives strategy traction. Clear values guide decision-making. Consistent leadership builds trust. Accountability reinforces discipline. Shared purpose strengthens commitment. In that environment, strategy becomes more than a document. It becomes a lived direction.

Culture always wins because it operates every day, in every conversation, in every decision, and in every moment of pressure. Strategy may change annually. Culture operates constantly. If leaders want a strategy to succeed, they must first build a culture capable of carrying it.

Strategy tells an organization where it intends to go. Culture determines whether it ever arrives.

Culture As Witness And Reputation

In a Christian organization, culture is more than an internal environment. It is a public testimony. It is how faith is seen, felt, and experienced by the people who encounter the organization. Culture becomes a living witness of what leaders truly believe, not merely what they claim. Long before a mission statement is read or a sermon is heard, culture has already spoken.

Jesus taught that a tree is known by its fruit. In the same way, an organization is known by its culture. The way people are treated, how conflict is handled, how money is managed, how truth is spoken, and how authority is exercised all communicate the organization's character. Culture either confirms or contradicts the gospel message.

The early church provides a powerful model of culture as witness. Acts 2:42–47 describes a community marked by devotion to teaching, fellowship, generosity, prayer, and unity. Their shared life was so compelling that Scripture says they had favor with all the people, and the Lord added to their number daily. Their culture was not created through branding or marketing. It was formed through obedience, love, and faithful leadership. Their reputation opened doors for the gospel.

Nehemiah offers another example. When he rebuilt the walls of Jerusalem, the surrounding nations mocked and threatened the work. Yet when the wall was completed, Scripture says the nations recognized that the work had been accomplished with God's help.

The people's discipline, unity, and perseverance under pressure became a testimony of God's faithfulness. Their culture of obedience and courage became a witness to the power of God.

In contrast, Scripture also shows how damaged culture destroys witness. When Israel tolerated injustice, corruption, and idolatry, their reputation among the nations suffered. God's name was dishonored because of the behavior of His people. The failure was not in doctrine. It was in daily conduct.

The same principle applies today. Churches and Christian organizations do not lose credibility because of theological disagreement. They lose credibility due to hypocrisy, financial misconduct, abuse of authority, favoritism, and a lack of accountability. When culture is compromised, witness is weakened. When culture is healthy, reputation is strengthened.

A Christ-centered culture reflects humility, integrity, compassion, discipline, and truth. It shows that leadership is servant-hearted, decisions are prayerful, and people are valued. When outsiders encounter such a culture, they encounter a visible expression of the gospel.

Chapter 9: Strategy

Directional Movement with Integrity

How Culture Becomes Movement →

Strategy is the bridge between belief and action. It is the disciplined process that turns culture into coordinated movement. Culture defines how people think and behave. Strategy defines how that shared behavior is directed toward a common objective. When culture is strong and aligned, strategy gives it momentum. When culture is weak or fragmented, strategy stalls before it ever reaches execution.

Culture creates readiness. It establishes trust, sets expectations, fosters accountability, and establishes shared language. Strategy then channels that readiness into an organized effort. A healthy culture produces people who are willing to move together. A clear strategy gives them direction for that movement. When both are present, organizations do not merely operate; they advance.

In Scripture, movement always followed alignment. When Nehemiah rebuilt the wall, the people did not begin with construction plans alone. They began with repentance, prayer, and renewed commitment to God. Their culture was restored before their strategy was deployed. Once alignment was established, the work advanced at a steady pace, with discipline and unity. The wall was completed in fifty-two days because the people shared conviction, commitment, and direction.

The early church followed the same pattern. Their culture was shaped by devotion to teaching, prayer, generosity, and fellowship. That culture produced boldness, obedience, and sacrifice. Strategy then emerged through intentional outreach, leadership development, missionary sending, and church planting.

What began as a community of believers became a global movement because culture and strategy moved together.

In organizations, culture determines whether strategy mobilizes or stagnates. A culture of trust accelerates execution. A culture of fear slows it. A culture of accountability drives results. A culture of apathy undermines them. Strategy cannot overcome culture. It must build upon it.

When leaders align values, vision, mission, and culture, strategy becomes a force multiplier. Decisions are made faster. Priorities are clearer. Resources are deployed more effectively. People know what matters and why it matters. Energy is focused rather than scattered.

Movement occurs when people are unified around a purpose and directed by clear priorities. Strategy provides the structure for that movement. Culture supplies the fuel. Together they create momentum that sustains growth, advances mission, and multiplies impact.

A strong culture without a strategy produces good intentions without progress. Strategy without culture produces plans without power. When culture and strategy are aligned, organizations move forward with conviction, clarity, and purpose.

What Strategy Really Is

Strategy is the intentional design of movement. It is the disciplined process of determining how an organization will move from its present position toward its future vision while faithfully executing its mission. Strategy is not a collection of ideas, initiatives, or aspirations. It is a coherent, prioritized, and resourced plan that directs people, time, and capital toward a defined destination.

Strategy begins with clarity. It requires leaders to understand where the organization is, where it is going, and what must be done to close the distance between the two. It identifies priorities, sequences actions, and allocates resources in a way that advances purpose rather than dispersing effort. A true strategy makes clear what the organization will pursue and what it will intentionally decline.

Strategy is directional, not reactive. It is not driven solely by urgency, pressure, or opportunity. Vision, values, and mission drive it. It ensures that decisions are made in alignment with long-term purpose rather than short-term convenience. It protects leaders from distraction and drift by providing a framework for evaluating every major initiative, partnership, and investment.

Strategy is also operational. It translates belief into execution. It turns conviction into action and culture into coordinated effort. It establishes timelines, responsibilities, measurements, and accountability. It defines how progress will be tracked and how adjustments will be made without abandoning direction.

Biblically, strategy reflects wise stewardship. Scripture consistently affirms that preparation, planning, and counsel are marks of faithful leadership. Leaders are called to count the cost, build with wisdom, and steward resources responsibly. Strategy is not a lack of faith. It is an expression of obedience, diligence, and responsibility.

An organization without a strategy may possess strong values, compelling vision, and sincere mission, yet still fail to advance. Without a strategy, effort becomes scattered, momentum fades, and potential remains unrealized. With strategy, purpose becomes progress, and conviction becomes movement. Strategy is the means by which leadership turns belief into results.

Strategy Versus Activity

Strategy and activity are not the same, though they are often confused. Activity is motion. Strategy is direction. Activity fills calendars, consumes energy, and produces visible effort. Strategy determines whether that effort advances the organization toward its vision or merely keeps it busy.

Organizations can be highly active and yet strategically stagnant. Meetings can be full. Programs can be running. Projects can be moving. Metrics can be reported. Budgets can be spent. Staff can be exhausted. None of these guarantees progress. Activity answers the question, "What are we doing?" Strategy answers the question, "Why are we doing it, and where is it taking us?"

Strategy disciplines activity. It provides the filter through which leaders evaluate initiatives, requests, and opportunities. It determines which actions deserve investment and which distractions must be declined. Without a strategy, organizations say yes too often and pursue too much. With strategy, leaders choose intentionally, sequencing effort according to purpose and capacity.

Activity responds to the present. Strategy prepares for the future. Activity reacts to urgency. Strategy advances toward the destination. Activity can create the illusion of progress. Strategy produces measurable movement.

Biblically, wisdom distinguishes between effort and effectiveness. Scripture repeatedly affirms that diligence without direction leads to waste, while counsel and planning establish success. Faithful leadership does not confuse motion with obedience or busyness with stewardship.

An organization driven by activity will eventually burn out. An organization guided by strategy builds momentum. Strategy ensures that every action serves the mission, honors the values, and advances the vision. Activity fills the day. Strategy shapes the future.

Strategic Focus And Restraint

Strategic focus is the discipline of choosing what matters most and committing organizational energy to those priorities with consistency and resolve. Restraint is the equally important discipline of saying no to distractions, detours, and opportunities that do not advance the mission or serve the vision. Together, focus and restraint form the guardrails of effective strategy.

Organizations often fail strategically not because they lack ideas, but because they lack discipline. Every new opportunity feels urgent. Every request feels important. Every trend appears promising. Without restraint, leaders chase momentum rather than building it. Resources are spread thin. Teams become reactive. Direction becomes blurred. The organization drifts from its core purpose while remaining constantly busy.

Strategic focus aligns effort with destination. It clarifies which initiatives deserve investment, which projects require patience, and which pursuits must be declined. It protects the organization from fragmentation and preserves energy for the work that truly advances the mission. Focus transforms good intentions into sustained progress.

Restraint protects integrity. It prevents leaders from compromising values for growth, visibility, or short-term gain. It ensures that expansion does not outpace capacity, that ambition does not override stewardship, and that speed does not replace wisdom. Restraint is not weakness. It is a strength exercised through self-governance and discernment.

Biblically, restraint is a mark of wisdom. Scripture teaches that success is not found in haste, excess, or impulsive action, but in counsel, patience, and obedience. Leaders are called not merely to act, but to act rightly. Focus and restraint allow leaders to build organizations that endure rather than collapse under the weight of unmanaged growth.

Strategic focus determines where the organization is going. Strategic restraint determines whether it will arrive with integrity, strength, and sustainability.

Resource Alignment

Resource alignment is the disciplined stewardship of people, time, capital, systems, and influence in direct support of the organization's values, vision, and mission. Strategy fails when resources are disconnected from priorities. Alignment succeeds when every major investment advances the same destination.

Organizations rarely fail because they lack resources. They fail because resources are misdirected. Talent is assigned to the wrong work. Time is consumed by low-impact activity. Budgets fund momentum instead of mission. Systems are built around convenience rather than clarity. When resources are scattered, strategy becomes theoretical rather than operational.

Aligned organizations deploy resources intentionally. People are placed where their gifts create the greatest impact. Time is protected for the work that matters most. Capital is invested where long-term value is created. Systems are designed to support execution rather than create friction. Influence is used to reinforce priorities, not dilute them.

Resource alignment also creates organizational trust. Teams gain confidence when they see leadership investing consistently in stated priorities. Cynicism grows when leaders talk about vision but fund something else. Credibility is built when decisions, budgets, hiring, training, and infrastructure reflect the same strategic commitments.

Biblically, stewardship is not optional. Scripture teaches that leaders are accountable for how they manage what has been entrusted to them. Wise stewardship multiplies impact. Neglect and mismanagement produce loss. Alignment honors God by treating every resource as a responsibility rather than a possession.

When resources follow strategy, organizations move with clarity and momentum. When strategy follows resources, organizations drift into survival mode. Resource alignment turns vision into movement and mission into measurable progress.

Sustainability Planning →

Sustainability planning is the discipline of building an organization that can endure, adapt, and remain faithful to its purpose over time. It is the long-term expression of stewardship, ensuring that today's success does not become tomorrow's collapse. Sustainability is not about growth for its own sake. It is about health, resilience, and faithful continuity across generations.

Many organizations experience short-lived seasons of momentum that fade because no structure is in place to carry the weight of success. Growth without sustainability creates exhaustion. Expansion without stability creates fragility. Innovation without endurance creates volatility. Sustainability planning asks a different set of questions. It asks whether the organization can remain faithful under pressure, survive leadership transitions, and continue serving its people with integrity ten, twenty, and fifty years from now.

Sustainable organizations plan beyond personalities. They build systems that outlast founders. They document processes so wisdom is transferable. They develop leaders, thereby multiplying authority. They protect culture so that values remain intact. They maintain financial discipline so resources are available when needed most. Sustainability is not accidental. It is designed.

From a biblical perspective, sustainability reflects faithful stewardship. Scripture consistently calls leaders to build wisely, to plan carefully, and to prepare for seasons of challenge. The parable of the talents teaches that what is entrusted must be multiplied, not merely preserved. Joseph's leadership in Egypt demonstrates the wisdom of preparing in seasons of abundance for seasons of famine. Sustainable leadership thinks beyond the present moment and acts with future responsibility.

Sustainability planning also guards mission integrity. When organizations lack long-term structure, they become reactive. Urgency replaces wisdom. Crisis replaces clarity. Pressure replaces prayer. Sustainable organizations remain anchored because their systems were built before the storm arrived.

Strategy creates movement. Sustainability ensures that movement can continue. When sustainability is ignored, success becomes temporary. When sustainability is planned, impact becomes lasting.

Why Strategy Fails

Strategy fails when treated as a document rather than a discipline. Many organizations invest significant time crafting plans, goals, and initiatives, yet see little lasting impact because strategy is not embedded into leadership behavior, decision-making systems, and organizational culture. A strategy that lives only on paper will never shape reality.

One of the most common reasons a strategy fails is misalignment. When values, vision, mission, culture, and policy are not integrated, strategy becomes disconnected from the organization's identity. Leaders may pursue initiatives that look impressive but do not serve the organization's true purpose. Teams become confused about priorities. Resources are spread thin. Energy is wasted on competing agendas. Without alignment, strategy becomes noise instead of direction.

Strategy also fails when it is driven by urgency rather than clarity. Reactive leadership produces short-term fixes instead of long-term solutions. Organizations begin chasing trends, copying competitors, or responding to every opportunity without discernment. This creates motion without progress and activity without impact. Strategic focus gives way to constant redirection, and momentum collapses under its own weight.

Another cause of failure is the absence of cultural support. Culture determines whether a strategy can live. If leadership behavior contradicts the plan, the plan will fail. If accountability is weak, execution will stall. If discipline is absent, priorities will drift. If trust is broken, commitment will fade. Strategy cannot overcome a dysfunctional culture. It must be carried by it.

Strategy fails when leadership does not own it. Delegating strategy without governance creates fragmentation. Leaders must model strategic discipline, reinforce priorities, protect focus, and make difficult tradeoffs. When leadership sends mixed signals, the organization follows confusion instead of direction.

From a biblical perspective, strategy fails when planning is separated from wisdom, prayer, and stewardship. Scripture teaches that wise counsel, discernment, and obedience to God's direction are essential for building anything that lasts. When leaders rely solely on human insight and ignore spiritual discernment, even well-designed plans can collapse.

A successful strategy is not built on clever ideas. It is built on aligned convictions, disciplined leadership, healthy culture, and faithful execution. When any of those foundations is missing, strategy becomes a temporary effort rather than a sustained movement.

The Danger of Reactionary Leadership

Reactionary leadership occurs when decisions are driven by pressure rather than purpose, by urgency rather than wisdom, and by fear rather than conviction. It is leadership that responds to the loudest voice, the latest crisis, or the most visible opportunity rather than to a clearly defined strategy anchored in values, vision, and mission. When leaders operate reactively, the organization loses direction and begins to drift from its intended destination.

Reactionary leadership creates instability. Priorities shift constantly. Initiatives are started and abandoned. Teams become uncertain about what truly matters. Employees learn to wait for the next change rather than commit fully to the current direction. Over time, momentum erodes because no effort is sustained long enough to produce meaningful results.

This form of leadership also weakens credibility. When leaders frequently change course, people stop trusting long-term plans. They become hesitant to invest their energy, creativity, and loyalty into initiatives that may be discarded tomorrow. Confidence in leadership declines as consistency gives way to unpredictability.

Reactionary leadership is often fueled by external pressure. Leaders feel compelled to respond to competitors, market trends, donor demands, public opinion, or internal complaints without first filtering those pressures through the organization's purpose and direction. Instead of asking whether an opportunity aligns with the mission and vision, leaders ask whether it will relieve immediate tension. The organization begins to chase relevance rather than pursue faithfulness.

Biblically, reactionary leadership reflects a lack of discernment and restraint. Scripture consistently calls leaders to seek wisdom, counsel, and God's direction before acting. Hasty decisions lead to regret, division, and wasted resources. Wise leadership requires patience, prayer, and clarity of calling.

Strategic leadership is proactive, not reactive. It anticipates challenges. It prepares for change. It filters opportunity through purpose. It chooses restraint as often as it chooses action. It understands that not every good idea is a God-directed assignment.

When leaders allow pressure to replace purpose, the organization loses its compass. When leaders remain anchored in values, vision, and mission, they lead with stability, confidence, and direction even in uncertain times.

Strategy As Stewardship

Strategy is not merely a plan for growth, expansion, or efficiency. It is a form of stewardship. It is the intentional, disciplined management of the people, resources, opportunities, and influence that God has entrusted to leadership. Strategic leadership recognizes that organizations do not own their mission. They are caretakers of a calling.

From a biblical perspective, stewardship is a sacred responsibility. Scripture teaches that everything belongs to God and that leaders are accountable for how they manage what has been entrusted to them. Strategy, therefore, is not about building personal platforms, protecting comfort, or chasing recognition. It is about faithfully multiplying what God has entrusted for His purposes.

In this sense, strategy becomes an act of obedience. It asks not only what can be done, but what should be done. It evaluates opportunities not solely by potential gain, but also by alignment with calling, values, and mission. It considers long-term impact rather than short-term success. It seeks sustainability rather than speed.

A stewardship-based strategy begins with clarity of purpose. Leaders must understand why their organization exists before determining how it should grow. When the purpose is clear, strategy becomes focused. When the purpose is unclear, strategy becomes scattered. Without stewardship, organizations accumulate programs, initiatives, and partnerships that consume resources without advancing the mission.

Stewardship also requires restraint. Faithful leaders recognize that saying yes to every opportunity is not faithfulness. It is often a distraction. Strategic restraint protects people from burnout, preserves financial health, and guards organizational focus. It ensures that energy is invested where it will produce lasting fruit rather than temporary visibility.

In Scripture, Jesus repeatedly modeled stewardship in leadership. He did not attempt to meet every need personally. He invested deeply in a small group, prepared them for multiplication, and entrusted them with responsibility. His strategy was not reactionary. It was intentional, relational, and long-term. He stewarded time, influence, and authority with purpose and discipline.

The apostle Paul demonstrated the same principle. His missionary journeys were not random. They were strategic. He identified key cities, developed leaders, established churches, and returned to strengthen them. His ministry reflects deliberate planning guided by the Holy Spirit and anchored in a clear mission.

When leaders approach strategy as stewardship, decision-making changes, and resources are allocated with care. People are developed with intention. Opportunities are evaluated with discernment. Growth is pursued with humility. Success is measured by faithfulness, not just results.

Stewardship-centered strategy honors God, protects the organization, and serves the people entrusted to leadership. It transforms planning from a business exercise into a spiritual responsibility and ensures that organizational movement remains aligned with God's purpose rather than driven by human ambition.

Chapter 10: Policy

Protecting Alignment Through Governance

What Policy Really Is →

Policy is the protective framework of leadership. It is the system that preserves values, safeguards culture, and stabilizes strategy over time. While vision defines direction and strategy defines movement, policy defines boundaries. It establishes what will be required, what will be protected, and what will be enforced. Without policy, organizational misalignment occurs. With policy, organizations endure.

Policy is not bureaucracy. It is stewardship. It is the formal expression of conviction applied to real leadership situations. It exists to protect people, preserve trust, and sustain integrity. In faith-based leadership, policy is not merely operational. It is moral. It reflects obedience to God's standards and responsibility toward those entrusted to leadership care.

Scripture consistently affirms that order, accountability, and structure are essential to faithful leadership. God is not a God of confusion, but of peace and order. Leadership that reflects His character must be governed by clarity, discipline, and consistency.

"For God is not a God of confusion but of peace." 1 Corinthians 14:33 (ESV)

Policy protects the organization from slow erosion, from the misalignment that occurs when standards are assumed rather than defined, when accountability is selective, and when expectations are left to personal interpretation. Organizational misalignment rarely happens suddenly. It occurs gradually through small compromises, unaddressed violations, and inconsistent leadership responses. Over time, values weaken, culture fragments, and trust erodes. Policy exists to prevent that outcome.

Culture reflects what people believe is acceptable. Strategy reflects what leaders intend to accomplish. The policy ensures that both are protected when pressure, growth, conflict, or crisis arise. It translates values into standards and transforms expectations into an enforceable structure. It provides continuity across leadership transitions, seasons of change, and organizational growth.

Biblically, leadership is always accompanied by responsibility and accountability. Scripture teaches that leaders are stewards who will give an account for how they care for people, resources, and influence.

"Moreover, it is required of stewards that they be found faithful." 1 Corinthians 4:2 (ESV)

Faithfulness is not abstract. It is demonstrated through disciplined leadership, clear standards, and consistent enforcement. Policy provides the mechanism for that faithfulness. It ensures that righteousness is not merely preached but practiced. It guards against favoritism, protects against abuse, and provides clarity when difficult decisions must be made.

Policy also reinforces organizational trust. When people know what is expected, what is protected, and how decisions are made, confidence grows. When policy is absent or inconsistently applied, confusion spreads. People begin to question motives, fairness, and the integrity of leadership.

Research supports this principle. Lucas (2018) demonstrated that clarity in organizational statements and leadership communication is directly connected to customer satisfaction and organizational health. When expectations are clearly defined and consistently applied, trust increases. When they are vague or unstable, satisfaction declines and alignment weakens. Policy functions as the operational extension of that clarity, ensuring that values and direction are not only stated but sustained.

Policy does not replace leadership judgment. It supports it. It provides a framework for leaders to exercise wisdom, discernment, and care. It allows organizations to grow without losing control, to innovate without losing integrity, and to adapt without losing identity.

In the LCSM10 framework, policy is the final protective layer. It guards what values establish, what vision directs, what mission defines, what culture shapes, and what strategy executes. It ensures that belief becomes behavior and that behavior remains faithful. Policy is how organizations honor God, protect people, and preserve purpose. It is not about restriction. It is about responsibility. It is leadership that refuses to accept misalignment at any level.

Policy Is How Belief Becomes Protection →

Policy is how belief becomes protection. It is the mechanism that transforms conviction into structure and turns values into enforceable standards. While values define what an organization believes and culture reveals how those beliefs are lived, policy ensures that those beliefs are preserved when pressure, growth, conflict, or crisis arise. Without policy, leadership depends on personality, memory, and preference. With policy, leadership operates with clarity, consistency, and accountability.

Policy exists to protect what matters most. It safeguards people from abuse, favoritism, and confusion. It preserves trust by establishing clear expectations and fair processes. It stabilizes organizations through seasons of transition, expansion, and uncertainty. When standards are written, communicated, and consistently applied, people know what is expected, what is protected, and how decisions are made. Confidence grows because leadership is predictable, principled, and accountable.

Biblically, protection through structure is not optional. God governs His people through law, covenant, and command, not to restrict life, but to preserve it. Order, accountability, and discipline are marks of faithful leadership. Scripture teaches that God is not a God of confusion, but of peace, and that all things are to be done decently and in order. Leadership that reflects His character must therefore be governed by clarity, consistency, and responsibility.

Policy prevents the slow erosion that occurs when standards are assumed rather than defined, when accountability is selective, and when expectations are left to personal interpretation. Organizational misalignment occurs gradually through small compromises, unaddressed violations, and inconsistent leadership responses. Over time, values weaken, culture fragments, and trust erodes. Policy exists to stop that process before it begins.

In the LCSM10 framework, policy is the final protective layer of organizational alignment. It guards what values establish, what vision directs, what mission defines, what culture shapes, and what strategy executes. It ensures that belief does not remain theoretical but becomes operational. It is how organizations honor God, protect people, and preserve purpose over time.

Policy As Stabilizing Boundaries

Policy functions as guardrails for leadership. It does not exist to restrict movement, but to keep the organization on the road that values, vision, mission, culture, and strategy have defined. Just as guardrails on a mountain highway do not limit the destination but prevent disaster along the way, policy protects the organization from veering into risk, abuse, confusion, or compromise. It provides boundaries that allow leaders to move forward with confidence, knowing that the organization is safeguarded from preventable failure.

Guardrails exist because danger is real. Every organization faces pressure from growth, financial strain, conflict, competition, legal exposure, and moral temptation. In these moments, decisions are often rushed, emotions are heightened, and shortcuts become appealing. Policy provides a stabilizing framework that keeps leadership anchored to principle rather than impulse. It ensures that urgency does not override integrity and that opportunity does not compromise responsibility.

In Scripture, God consistently establishes boundaries to protect His people. The law, the commandments, and the wisdom literature all function as guardrails designed to preserve life, justice, and righteousness. These were not given to limit freedom, but to direct it toward blessing and stability. Similarly, organizational policy is an expression of stewardship. It protects people from harm, protects leaders from isolation, and protects the mission from corruption.

Policy as guardrails also protects unity. When standards are clear and consistently applied, leaders are not forced to negotiate expectations in every situation. Decisions are not made based on favoritism, emotion, or power. They are made according to shared conviction and agreed-upon structure. This builds trust across teams and prevents the fragmentation that results from exercising authority without accountability.

In the LCSM10 framework, policy guardrails preserve alignment. They ensure that culture remains healthy, strategy remains disciplined, and leadership remains faithful. Policy does not replace wisdom. It supports it. It does not remove discernment. It strengthens it. Policy allows organizations to move forward with courage, clarity, and confidence, knowing that belief has been translated into protection and that leadership is operating within boundaries that honor God and serve people well.

Ethics And Accountability

Ethics and accountability form the moral backbone of organizational leadership. They ensure that power is exercised with integrity, decisions are made with honesty, and authority is carried with responsibility. Ethics define what is right. Accountability ensures that what is right is practiced. Together, they prevent leadership from drifting into self-interest, favoritism, secrecy, or abuse.

Ethics are not situational. They are not shaped by convenience, profit, or pressure. They are rooted in truth and governed by conviction. In faith-based leadership, ethics are grounded in obedience to God and reverence for His standards.

Leaders do not simply answer to boards, customers, or shareholders. They answer to God for how they steward people, resources, and influence. Scripture teaches that leadership is a trust, not a privilege, and that every steward will one day give an account.

Accountability is the structure that protects ethical leadership from erosion. It provides transparency, oversight, and correction. It ensures that no leader operates in isolation, no decision escapes review, and no authority is unchecked. Accountability does not signal distrust. It demonstrates wisdom. It recognizes that even well-intentioned leaders are vulnerable to blind spots, pressure, and temptation.

Biblically, accountability is a consistent theme. Leaders are called to walk in the light, to submit to counsel, and to welcome correction. The absence of accountability always produces vulnerability. When leaders are unaccountable, organizations become fragile. When accountability is present, trust grows and culture strengthens.

Ethics and accountability also protect the people being led. They safeguard against exploitation, manipulation, and injustice. They create environments where fairness is expected, truth is honored, and wrongdoing is addressed rather than hidden. This builds confidence in leadership and organizational stability.

Within the LCSM10 framework, ethics and accountability serve as the moral enforcement mechanism of policy. They ensure that values are not symbolic, that culture is not performative, and that strategy is not reckless. They preserve organizational integrity under pressure and provide the discipline necessary for long-term sustainability.

When ethics guide leadership and accountability governs authority, organizations endure. Trust is preserved. Culture remains healthy. Purpose is protected. Leadership becomes credible. This is how belief becomes behavior and how conviction becomes organizational strength.

Governance And Authority

Governance and authority define how leadership power is structured, exercised, and restrained within an organization. Governance establishes who has decision-making responsibility, how authority is distributed, and how leadership is held accountable. Authority provides the capacity to lead, direct, correct, and protect. Together, governance and authority form the framework that preserves order, legitimacy, and trust.

Authority is not control. It is stewardship. Leadership authority exists for the good of those being led, not for personal advantage or institutional dominance. Scripture consistently presents authority as a responsibility entrusted by God, not a privilege seized by ambition. Leaders are called to shepherd, serve, and protect, not dominate. When authority is exercised faithfully, it produces stability, unity, and confidence. When it is abused or left undefined, confusion and division follow.

Governance provides the structure that keeps authority aligned with purpose and values. It defines roles, responsibilities, reporting relationships, and decision boundaries. It ensures that leadership is not centralized in unchecked power, but distributed with wisdom, accountability, and clarity. Good governance protects the organization from personality-driven leadership, emotional decision-making, and reactionary control.

Biblically, governance is modeled throughout Scripture. Moses was given elders and judges to share leadership responsibility. David ruled with counselors and commanders. The early church appointed apostles, elders, and deacons to ensure order, care, and oversight. These structures were not created to slow the mission, but to protect it. They allowed God's work to advance without collapsing into disorder.

Authority without governance becomes authoritarian. Governance without authority becomes ineffective. Healthy organizations require both. Leaders must be empowered to lead, and structure, counsel, and accountability must restrain leadership. This balance preserves moral clarity, protects people, and sustains long-term organizational health.

Within the LCSM10 framework, governance and authority function as stabilizing forces within policy. They ensure that leadership remains aligned with values, remains faithful to the vision, remains focused on the mission, and remains accountable for culture and strategy. They prevent organizational misalignment by anchoring leadership to structure and conviction.

When governance is clear, and authority is exercised with humility and discipline, organizations operate with confidence and integrity. Decisions are trusted. Direction is respected. Leadership becomes credible. Power is no longer feared or questioned because it is visibly governed by purpose, accountability, and faithfulness before God.

Discipline And Restoration

Discipline and restoration are essential expressions of faithful leadership. They protect the integrity of the organization, safeguard people from harm, and preserve the moral and spiritual health of the community. Discipline is not punishment for failure. It is a correction for growth. Restoration is not tolerance of sin. It is redemption through repentance. Together, they reflect the heart of God toward His people and the responsibility of leaders to steward truth with grace.

Discipline exists because leadership is accountable before God for the people entrusted to its care. Scripture teaches that love does not ignore sin and that grace does not excuse disobedience. Faithful leadership confronts what is harmful, addresses what is broken, and corrects what threatens the body's health. Discipline establishes boundaries, clarifies expectations, and reinforces responsibility. It communicates that conduct, character, and obedience matter.

At the same time, discipline is never an end in itself. Its purpose is restoration. God's design is not condemnation, but repentance and renewal. Restoration reflects the gospel itself. Christ confronts sin, but He also offers forgiveness, healing, and transformation. Leadership that disciplines without offering restoration becomes harsh and legalistic. Leadership that offers restoration without discipline becomes permissive and unsafe. Biblical leadership holds both together.

Scripture provides a clear model for discipline and restoration. Jesus outlined a process of correction rooted in truth, humility, and accountability. The goal is not humiliation, but reconciliation. The apostle Paul instructed the church to confront sin for the protection of the body, and later urged restoration when repentance was demonstrated. Discipline guarded the community. Restoration healed the individual.

Discipline protects culture. It reinforces values. It defends trust. When leaders fail to address misconduct, compromise becomes normal, and integrity erodes. Over time, silence becomes approval, and tolerance becomes endorsement. Restoration protects people. It communicates that failure is not final, that repentance is honored, and that transformation is possible. Together, discipline and restoration preserve both holiness and hope.

Within organizational policy, discipline provides the standard for conduct and the process for correction. Restoration provides the pathway for redemption and reintegration. These systems ensure that leadership remains consistent, fair, and faithful. They protect against favoritism, retaliation, and emotional decision-making. They ensure that justice is applied with wisdom and mercy.

In the LCSM10 framework, discipline and restoration function as guardians of alignment. They preserve values, protect culture, and stabilize strategy under pressure. They ensure that belief becomes behavior and that behavior remains accountable to God's truth.

Leadership that practices discipline with humility and restoration with compassion reflects the character of Christ. It produces organizations that are safe, credible, and trustworthy. It builds cultures where righteousness is honored, repentance is respected, and grace is lived. This is not weak leadership. It is courageous leadership. It is leadership that refuses to misalign and chooses faithfulness instead.

Why Organizations Avoid Policy →

Organizations often avoid policy because it feels restrictive, confrontational, or inconvenient. Leaders fear that formal standards will slow momentum, limit flexibility, or create resistance. In fast-moving environments, policy is frequently viewed as an obstacle rather than a safeguard. As a result, many organizations operate on assumptions, informal norms, and personal judgment rather than on clear, written governance.

One of the most common reasons organizations avoid policy is discomfort with accountability. Policy requires leaders to define expectations, establish boundaries, and enforce standards consistently. This removes the option of selective enforcement and forces leadership to address difficult issues directly. Confrontation becomes unavoidable. Hard conversations become necessary. Decisions must be justified by principle rather than preference. For leaders who prefer harmony over clarity, or popularity over responsibility, policy feels threatening.

Another reason policy is avoided is the false belief that a strong culture makes formal structure unnecessary. When an organization experiences early success, close relationships, or shared passion, leaders often assume that values alone will sustain alignment. Over time, however, growth introduces complexity. New people join. Pressure increases. Decisions carry greater consequences. Without policy, culture becomes vulnerable to erosion, favoritism, and inconsistency.

Some organizations resist policy because they associate it with bureaucracy rather than stewardship. They confuse order with control and structure with rigidity. Policy does not exist to restrict healthy leadership. It exists to protect it. It provides clarity when emotions are high, stability when pressure is intense, and consistency during leadership transitions. Without policy, every crisis becomes a negotiation. Every conflict becomes personal. Every failure becomes subjective.

There is also a spiritual dimension to policy avoidance in faith-based leadership. Many leaders desire to lead with grace and compassion, but struggle to balance mercy with truth. In an effort to avoid appearing judgmental or harsh, they hesitate to define boundaries or enforce standards. Over time, however, the absence of discipline weakens culture, compromises integrity, and damages witness. Grace without truth becomes permissiveness. Love without accountability becomes neglect.

Scripture consistently affirms that faithful leadership requires structure, order, and responsibility. God established laws, covenants, and commands not to burden His people, but to protect them. In the same way, organizational policy is an expression of care, not control. It guards people from harm, leaders from compromise, and institutions from collapse.

Research supports this reality. Lucas (2018) demonstrated that clarity in organizational statements and leadership communication is directly connected to trust, satisfaction, and long-term effectiveness. When expectations are defined and enforced, confidence increases. When they are vague or inconsistent, alignment deteriorates, and credibility weakens.

Organizations that avoid policy often do so until failure forces change. A crisis exposes what was assumed. A scandal reveals what was ignored. A lawsuit exposes what was undefined. By the time the policy is written, damage has already been done.

Policy is not a sign of distrust. It is a sign of wisdom. It is leadership that anticipates pressure, prepares for growth, and refuses to move from written policy. Organizations that embrace policy do not become rigid. They become resilient.

The Cost of Weak Boundaries

Weak boundaries carry a cost that is rarely visible at first, but always devastating over time. When leadership fails to define and enforce clear standards, organizations slowly normalize compromise. Expectations become negotiable. Accountability becomes selective. Integrity becomes conditional. What was once unthinkable becomes tolerated, and what was once tolerated becomes accepted. Culture erodes not through rebellion, but through neglect. Boundaries exist to protect people, preserve trust, and prevent harm. When they are weak or undefined, confusion replaces clarity, favoritism replaces fairness, and personal interpretation replaces shared conviction.

In leadership, weak boundaries place an unfair burden on relationships. When standards are unclear, every decision becomes personal. Every correction feels like a personal attack. Every enforcement feels inconsistent. Staff, volunteers, and stakeholders are left guessing where the lines are, which creates anxiety, resentment, and distrust. Over time, morale declines, conflict increases, and credibility weakens. People do not feel safe in systems where expectations shift based on personality, pressure, or circumstance.

Weak boundaries also expose organizations to ethical failure. Most moral collapses do not begin with major transgressions. They begin with small compromises that go unchallenged. A financial shortcut. A private conversation that should not have happened. A conflict of interest that was ignored. A standard that was bent for the sake of convenience or a relationship. When boundaries are not enforced early, they are rarely restored later. Scripture warns that sin left unchecked grows, spreads, and destroys. Leadership that tolerates compromise eventually inherits its consequences.

In faith-based organizations, weak boundaries damage witness. The church is called to be distinct, holy, and set apart. When leaders avoid discipline, refuse accountability, or blur moral lines, the message of the gospel is undermined. Grace without truth becomes permissiveness. Love without correction becomes neglect. The result is not compassion, but confusion. Scripture teaches that those entrusted with leadership will give an account for how they steward people, influence, and authority. Boundaries are part of that stewardship.

Weak boundaries also weaken strategy and culture. Strategy depends on discipline. Culture depends on consistency. When standards are not protected, execution becomes unstable, and culture becomes fragmented. What leadership intends is no longer what the organization practices. Over time, alignment collapses, and misalignment becomes the norm.

Strong boundaries do not create harsh environments. They create healthy ones. They establish safety, fairness, and trust. They allow leaders to correct with clarity, discipline with compassion, and restore with integrity. Boundaries are not a sign of control. They are a sign of care. They are leaders who refuse to compromise or abandon responsibility.

Organizations with weak boundaries eventually pay a price in trust, reputation, morale, and mission. Organizations with strong boundaries endure.

Policy As Leadership Protection →

Policy functions as a form of leadership protection by establishing clear standards that safeguard both the organization and those entrusted with its care. It provides leaders with a defined framework for decision-making, accountability, and enforcement, ensuring that authority is exercised consistently, fairly, and with integrity. Without policy, leadership becomes vulnerable to personal pressure, emotional reaction, favoritism, and situational compromise. With policy, leadership is anchored to principle rather than personality.

Policy protects leaders from isolation by removing ambiguity from difficult decisions. When standards are clearly written and consistently applied, leaders are not forced to rely solely on personal judgment. Instead, they steward a shared framework that reflects organizational values, biblical conviction, and ethical responsibility. This allows correction, discipline, and restoration to be carried out with clarity and fairness rather than emotion or impulse.

In faith-based leadership, policy also protects spiritual authority. Scripture consistently affirms that leadership is a stewardship entrusted by God and exercised under His authority. Leaders are not owners of influence, but caretakers of people, resources, and mission. Policy provides the structure through which that stewardship is exercised faithfully, ensuring that authority is not abused and responsibility is not avoided when difficult decisions must be made.

Policy further protects leaders from burnout and moral fatigue. When expectations are undefined, every conflict becomes a crisis, and every violation becomes a negotiation. Over time, this erodes resolve and weakens courage. Policy establishes boundaries that allow leaders to lead with confidence, knowing that they are operating within a system designed to protect righteousness, fairness, and trust.

Leadership that is protected by policy is leadership that can remain faithful under pressure. It can correct without fear, decide without favoritism, and lead without compromise. Policy is not a limitation on leadership. It is a safeguard for it.

Chapter 11: CSPA

Culture–Strategy–Policy Alignment Model (LCSM10 – CSPA)
A Core Operational Model Within the LCSM10 Framework

Policy As Stabilizing Boundaries →

Locking the system together is the final act of organizational alignment. It is the point at which values, vision, mission, culture, strategy, and policy cease to function as independent ideas and begin operating as a single leadership system. When properly integrated, these elements no longer compete for attention or authority. They reinforce one another, creating a unified framework that governs decision-making, behavior, accountability, and long-term direction.

Organizations fail when leadership systems are built in fragments. Vision is written without values. Strategy is executed without culture. Policy is enforced without a mission. Culture is shaped without direction. When these elements are disconnected, leaders are forced to rely on personality, intuition, and reaction rather than principle, structure, and stewardship. Over time, inconsistency replaces clarity, pressure overrides conviction, and misalignment becomes inevitable.

The LCSM10 Culture–Strategy–Policy Alignment Model exists to prevent that outcome. It binds belief to behavior, direction to execution, and conviction to protection. Culture becomes the expression of what the organization truly believes. Strategy becomes the disciplined movement of those beliefs into action. Policy becomes the safeguard that preserves those beliefs when pressure, conflict, growth, or crisis arises.

When the system is locked together, leadership becomes coherent. Decisions follow a consistent logic. Authority is exercised with integrity. Accountability is applied with fairness. Resources are stewarded with purpose. Growth is pursued without compromise.

Innovation is encouraged without recklessness. Change is embraced without abandoning identity.

Scripture affirms this model of unified leadership. God does not govern His people through disconnected commands or fragmented authority. He establishes covenant, law, instruction, and order as a complete system of life and obedience. His design reflects alignment, structure, and accountability working together for protection and flourishing.

A house divided against itself cannot stand. A leadership system divided against itself will not endure.

When culture, strategy, and policy operate as a single system, the organization gains stability under pressure, clarity in decision-making, and resilience through transitions. Leaders no longer react to circumstances. They respond from conviction. They do not manage chaos. They govern with order. They do not chase opportunity. They pursue purpose.

Locking the system together is not about control. It is about stewardship. It is a conviction that refuses to compromise. It is a structure that refuses to fail. This is where belief becomes behavior. This is where direction becomes movement. This is where conviction becomes protection. This is where leadership becomes durable.

How Culture Drives Strategy

Culture drives strategy because strategy always follows what an organization truly believes, rewards, and tolerates. While strategy is often treated as a technical exercise involving goals, plans, and initiatives, it is ultimately a behavioral expression of culture. Culture determines what leaders prioritize, how decisions are made, what risks are accepted, and which opportunities are pursued. Strategy does not emerge in a vacuum. It emerges from the organization's collective mindset, convictions, and habits.

An organization may publish a strategy that appears disciplined, focused, and well-constructed, yet if the culture does not support execution, the strategy will fail. A culture that tolerates complacency will undermine a strategy that requires excellence. A culture that avoids accountability will weaken a strategy that depends on performance. A culture that resists change will sabotage a strategy built on innovation. Strategy is only as strong as the culture that carries it.

Culture shapes how leaders interpret information, evaluate threats, and respond to opportunities. It influences whether leaders act decisively or hesitate, whether they pursue long-term investment or short-term comfort, and whether they protect values or compromise under pressure. In this sense, culture serves as the organization's internal operating system. Strategy becomes the visible output of that system.

Biblically, this principle is consistently reinforced. Scripture teaches that behavior flows from the heart, and that direction follows conviction. Jesus taught that a good tree produces good fruit and a bad tree produces bad fruit. The nature of the tree determines the outcome. In the same way, organizational culture determines strategic direction. What leaders cultivate internally is what the organization produces externally. "Ye shall know them by their fruits." Matthew 7:16 (KJV)

When culture is healthy, strategy becomes focused, disciplined, and sustainable. Leaders pursue growth with integrity. Innovation is guided by stewardship. Expansion is governed by responsibility. When culture is weak, strategy becomes reactive, fragmented, and unstable. Leaders chase trends, imitate competitors, and pursue growth without discernment.

Culture also determines how the organization receives strategy. In a culture of trust, strategy inspires commitment. In a culture of fear, strategy produces resistance. In a culture of unity, strategy mobilizes action. In a culture of fragmentation, strategy creates confusion.

Within the LCSM10 framework, culture is the engine that drives strategic movement. Values establish conviction. Vision defines destination. Mission clarifies purpose. Culture forms behavior. Strategy channels that behavior into disciplined action. When culture is aligned with values, vision, and mission, strategy becomes the natural expression of organizational identity rather than a forced initiative.

Organizations do not execute strategies. People do. People act according to what they believe is expected, rewarded, and protected. Culture determines that belief system. Strategy follows.

When culture is formed intentionally, strategy becomes powerful. When culture is neglected, strategy becomes performative. Leadership does not move organizations forward through plans alone. It moves them forward through people who believe, belong, and align with a shared conviction.

How Policy Protects Culture →

Policy protects culture by preserving standards when pressure, growth, conflict, or compromise threaten to weaken conviction. Culture reflects what people believe is acceptable. Policy ensures that what is acceptable is clearly defined, consistently enforced, and faithfully protected. Without policy, culture becomes vulnerable to erosion. With policy, culture gains durability.

Culture is formed through repeated behavior over time. What leaders reward becomes normal. What leaders tolerate becomes acceptable. What leaders ignore becomes embedded. Policy interrupts this misalignment by formalizing expectations and establishing accountability. It translates shared values into enforceable standards and transforms cultural conviction into organizational discipline.

An organization may claim to value integrity, accountability, stewardship, and excellence, yet without policy, those values remain aspirational. When pressure arises, when finances tighten, when influence grows, or when conflict emerges, values that are not protected by policy are easily compromised. Policy ensures that values remain operational rather than symbolic.

Policy also protects culture by creating consistency across leadership transitions and seasons of change. Leaders come and go. Markets shift. Ministries expand. Teams grow. Without policy, culture becomes dependent on personality rather than principle. Over time, inconsistency replaces alignment, and wavering behavior replaces direction. Policy provides continuity by anchoring culture to written standards rather than individual discretion.

Biblically, God governs His people through law, covenant, and command. These were not given to restrict obedience but to preserve righteousness. God's instructions provided clarity, accountability, and protection for His people so that faith would be lived faithfully across generations. In the same way, organizational policy exists to preserve what is right, protect what is good, and guard against corruption.

Scripture teaches that leadership carries responsibility and accountability. Leaders are stewards who must give an account for how they manage people, resources, and influence. Policy provides the structure for that stewardship. It ensures that authority is exercised justly, discipline is applied consistently, and restoration is pursued with wisdom.

Policy also protects people. It safeguards staff, volunteers, congregants, customers, and stakeholders from favoritism, abuse, confusion, and injustice. When expectations are clear and standards are enforced fairly, trust grows. When policy is absent or selectively applied, suspicion rises, and credibility erodes.

In healthy organizations, culture shapes behavior, and policy protects behavior. Culture provides identity. Policy provides security. Culture inspires commitment. Policy sustains integrity.

Together, they create an environment where leadership remains faithful under pressure and organizations remain aligned over time.

Within the LCSM10 framework, policy is the guardian of culture. It preserves what values establish, what vision directs, what mission defines, and what strategy executes. It ensures that belief does not remain theoretical and that conviction does not dissolve under pressure. Policy is how culture endures.

Alignment Under Pressure

Alignment under pressure reveals whether an organization is truly governed by conviction or merely guided by convenience. Pressure exposes the strength of leadership systems. When growth accelerates, resources tighten, conflict emerges, or reputation is tested, alignment is either reinforced or fractured. Organizations that have built their values, vision, mission, culture, strategy, and policy as an integrated system remain steady. Organizations that have built them as isolated concepts are prone to organizational misalignment.

Pressure does not create misalignment. It reveals it. When decisions must be made quickly, when finances are strained, when influence expands, or when public scrutiny intensifies, leaders default to their true operating framework. If values are not embedded, vision is not shared, mission is not operational, culture is not reinforced, and policy is not enforced, leadership begins to fragment. Authority becomes inconsistent. Standards weaken. Direction becomes reactive. Over time, the organization loses coherence.

Alignment under pressure requires more than strong personalities or inspirational leadership. It requires a system that holds when emotion is high, stakes are real, and consequences are costly. Values must already be defined. Vision must already be clear. Mission must already be operational. Culture must already be lived. Policy must already be in place. When pressure arrives, there is no time to build alignment. There is only time to rely on what already exists.

Biblically, pressure has always been the proving ground of leadership. Nehemiah faced opposition, intimidation, and political pressure while rebuilding the wall. Yet he refused to compromise the mission God had given him. He kept the people focused, resisted distraction, and guarded the work with vigilance and prayer. His leadership held because his vision was clear, his conviction was firm, and his boundaries were established before the pressure peaked.

Jesus also modeled alignment under pressure. When confronted with temptation, political manipulation, and public opposition, He remained anchored in the will of the Father. He did not adjust His mission to preserve popularity. He did not dilute truth to avoid conflict. He did not abandon His calling to protect His comfort. His leadership remained aligned because His identity, purpose, and obedience were settled long before the pressure arrived.

In organizational life, pressure comes in many forms. Rapid growth stretches systems. Financial strain tests integrity. Conflict challenges unity. Crisis exposes character. Cultural shifts demand discernment. Leadership fatigue invites compromise. Without alignment, pressure forces leaders into survival mode, where decisions are driven by urgency rather than conviction, and reaction replaces direction.

Aligned organizations respond differently. They do not panic. They do not fracture. They return to their values. They measure decisions against their vision. They evaluate opportunities through their mission. They protect their culture. They enforce their policies. Pressure becomes a proving ground rather than a breaking point.

Research consistently affirms this principle. Organizations with clear, aligned leadership systems demonstrate greater resilience, stronger trust, and higher performance under stress. Lucas (2018) demonstrated that clarity and consistency in organizational statements are directly connected to organizational health and stakeholder satisfaction. When alignment is strong, confidence increases. When alignment weakens, uncertainty spreads.

Alignment under pressure is not accidental. It is designed. It is built through disciplined leadership, intentional systems, and faithful stewardship. It is maintained through accountability, communication, and consistency. It is protected through policy and reinforced through culture.

In the LCSM10 framework, alignment under pressure is the ultimate test of leadership. It demonstrates whether belief has truly become behavior and whether structure has truly become strength. When the system is aligned, pressure does not divide. It refines.

Crisis Leadership →

Crisis leadership is the moment when leadership systems are tested to their limits. Crisis removes the luxury of delay, exposes hidden weaknesses, and demands immediate decision-making with long-term consequences. In these moments, leadership is no longer theoretical. It becomes visible, measurable, and definable.

A crisis does not create leadership character. It reveals it. When disruption strikes, whether through financial collapse, moral failure, public scandal, legal exposure, internal division, or external threat, leaders default to their true governing framework. If values are not embedded, vision is unclear, mission is not operational, culture is not healthy, and policy is not enforced, the crisis will magnify fragmentation. Authority will become unstable. Communication will become reactive. Decisions will become inconsistent. Trust will erode.

Crisis leadership requires more than courage. It requires alignment. Leaders must know who they are, what they stand for, where they are going, and how they are governed. Crisis compresses time and amplifies consequences. There is no space for improvisation, experimentation, or ambiguity. The organization must already be anchored.

Scripture repeatedly presents crisis as the proving ground of leadership. Joseph led Egypt through famine because God had given him foresight, wisdom, and preparation long before the crisis arrived. Moses led Israel through the Red Sea because God had already shaped his obedience, endurance, and faith in the wilderness. Nehemiah rebuilt Jerusalem under threat because his vision was clear, his mission was fixed, and his leadership was disciplined. Esther confronted genocide because she understood that her position carried responsibility for such a time as this.

Jesus Himself demonstrated the highest form of crisis leadership. In the final hours before the cross, He did not retreat from His mission. He did not abandon His calling. He did not negotiate His obedience. In the garden, under emotional, spiritual, and physical pressure, He submitted fully to the will of the Father. His leadership was not driven by survival, but by obedience.

In organizational life, a crisis reveals whether leadership is centered on preservation or purpose. Leaders who prioritize reputation over righteousness often conceal, deny, or deflect. Leaders who prioritize comfort over conviction compromise standards to quickly restore peace. Leaders who prioritize control over accountability isolate decision-making and silence dissent. These responses accelerate collapse rather than prevent it.

Faithful crisis leadership follows a different pattern. It returns to values. It tells the truth. It accepts responsibility. It protects people. It enforces standards. It communicates clearly. It acts decisively. It submits to accountability. It seeks wisdom. It remains steady.

A crisis also exposes whether culture is healthy or toxic. In a healthy culture, people rally around shared conviction, trust leadership, and move together toward restoration. In a toxic culture, fear spreads, factions form, rumors multiply, and loyalty collapses. Culture determines whether a crisis becomes a refining fire or a consuming one.

Policy becomes essential in a crisis. Policy provides clarity when emotions are high. It defines authority when power is contested. It protects fairness when pressure tempts favoritism. It ensures that decisions are governed by principle rather than panic. Policy is not restrictive in a crisis. It is stabilizing.

Strategy must also be adjusted in a crisis, but never abandoned. Crisis does not remove the need for direction. It heightens it. Leaders must know which priorities remain non-negotiable, which initiatives must pause, and which actions must accelerate. Strategy ensures that survival does not replace purpose.

Research consistently affirms that organizations with strong governance, clear leadership frameworks, and disciplined decision-making recover faster, retain trust, and sustain long-term performance following a crisis. Lucas (2018) demonstrated that clarity and consistency in leadership communication are directly connected to organizational confidence and satisfaction. In a crisis, clarity becomes even more critical.

Crisis leadership is not about heroics. It is about stewardship. It is leadership that refuses to waver when pressure is greatest. It is leadership that protects people when risk is highest. It is leadership that preserves integrity when compromise is tempting. It is leadership that stands firm when retreat would be easier. In the LCSM10 framework, crisis leadership is the moment when alignment proves its worth. Values guide judgment. Vision preserves direction. Mission sustains purpose. Culture maintains unity. Strategy restores momentum. Policy safeguards integrity. Crisis is not the end of leadership. It is the moment leadership is revealed.

Organizational Resilience →

Organizational resilience is the capacity to endure disruption without losing identity, direction, or integrity. It is not merely the ability to survive difficulty, but the ability to remain faithful, aligned, and effective when pressure, uncertainty, and adversity threaten stability. Resilience allows organizations to absorb shock, adapt with wisdom, and continue moving forward without compromising their convictions.

Resilience is built long before a crisis arrives. It is formed through disciplined leadership, clear values, stable culture, sound strategy, and enforced policy. Organizations that rely on personality, charisma, or momentum eventually fracture under pressure. Organizations that rely on alignment endure.

Resilient organizations know who they are. Values are not symbolic. They are governing convictions. Vision is not aspirational language. It is a fixed destination. Mission is not a slogan. It is a daily direction. Culture is not atmosphere. It is behavior. Strategy is not an activity. It is movement. Policy is not bureaucracy. It is protection.

When these elements are aligned, organizations gain internal strength. When one layer weakens, resilience begins to erode.

Scripture consistently affirms that endurance is a mark of faithful leadership. Jesus taught that those who build on the rock remain standing when storms come. Paul reminded the church that perseverance produces maturity. James taught that testing refines faith. Biblical leadership does not promise comfort. It promises endurance through obedience.

Joseph demonstrated resilience through betrayal, imprisonment, and political uncertainty. His leadership remained anchored in obedience and integrity, allowing God to use him to preserve a nation during famine. Nehemiah demonstrated resilience through opposition, intimidation, and exhaustion. His leadership remained anchored in vision and discipline, allowing God to rebuild a broken city. The early church demonstrated resilience through persecution, loss, and dispersion. Their mission remained anchored in Christ, allowing the gospel to spread throughout the world.

Resilience is not stubbornness. It is discernment. It is the ability to adapt methods without abandoning the mission. It is the discipline to change tactics without losing direction. It is the wisdom to innovate without eroding identity.

Resilient organizations plan for sustainability. They steward resources wisely. They develop leaders intentionally. They document standards clearly. They prepare for succession. They invest in systems that outlast personalities. They build redundancy, accountability, and continuity into their structure.

Culture plays a central role in resilience. In healthy cultures, people trust leadership, uphold standards, and protect unity. In unhealthy cultures, fear spreads, loyalty fractures, and survival replaces purpose. Culture determines whether adversity strengthens the organization or exposes its weaknesses.

Policy strengthens resilience by providing clarity during uncertainty. It preserves fairness under pressure. It protects people during conflict. It safeguards integrity during temptation. Policy ensures that leadership remains consistent even in unstable circumstances.

Strategy sustains resilience by preserving direction during disruption. When a crisis strikes, resilient organizations do not abandon their mission. They adjust their movement. They refine their priorities. They reallocate resources. They accelerate what matters most.

Research consistently affirms that organizations with strong governance, disciplined leadership systems, and clear communication recover faster from disruption and retain higher levels of trust. Lucas (2018) demonstrated that clarity and consistency in leadership communication are directly connected to organizational confidence and satisfaction. Resilient organizations communicate early, clearly, and truthfully.

Resilience is not the absence of hardship. It is the presence of alignment.

In the LCSM10 framework, resilience is the outcome of integration. Values provide moral stability. Vision provides directional stability. Mission provides operational stability. Culture provides relational stability. Strategy provides movement stability. Policy provides structural stability. When these layers operate as one system, organizations do not merely survive storms. They stand.

The Limits of Awareness and the Necessity of Construction

Organizational misalignment cannot be corrected by awareness alone. Leaders may clearly recognize misalignment, inefficiency, or internal contradiction, yet those conditions often persist even after they are named. Intention, motivation, and cultural emphasis can temporarily reduce symptoms, but they do not address the underlying structural causes of misalignment. Without a corrective structure, organizations tend to revert to prior patterns, even when leadership commitment remains sincere.

Attempts to resolve misalignment through renewed energy, inspirational messaging, or cultural reinforcement frequently fail because they operate at the level of behavior rather than at the level of design. Culture responds to structure, not the other way around. When values, vision, and mission lack coherence or are developed independently, no amount of reinforcement can sustain alignment. In such cases, effort increases while clarity does not.

Correction requires more than agreement on what is wrong. It requires deliberate reconstruction of the organizational statements that shape direction, priorities, and decision-making. This reconstruction must be intentional, sequenced, and constrained. Alignment does not emerge organically from discussion or consensus; it is the result of disciplined design.

The purpose of this framework has been to establish the language, logic, and conditions for accurately recognizing organizational misalignment. Recognition, however, is only the first responsibility of leadership. The second is execution. Moving forward requires a shift from understanding problems to constructing solutions, using methods that reduce ambiguity rather than amplify it.

PART IV

Preparing for Disciplined Organizational Statement Construction

This section marks the transition from framework to construction. The preceding chapters established the logic, language, and leadership architecture of the LCSM10 framework. Part IV prepares the reader to move from understanding alignment to deliberately building it.

This section introduces disciplined organizational statement construction as a leadership responsibility rather than a reflective exercise. Values, vision, and mission are no longer treated as expressive language but as structural instruments that must be intentionally designed, sequenced, and integrated to function as a unified system.

Chapter 12 establishes the necessity of disciplined construction and clarifies why alignment cannot be achieved through awareness, intention, or wording alone. What follows are the Creation and Integration Modules for values, vision, and mission. These modules provide the structured process required to construct organizational statements with coherence, constraint, and authority, and to integrate them so they operate together as a single leadership system.

Chapter 12: Disciplined Organizational Statement Construction

From Framework to Construction

Organizational misalignment cannot be corrected through awareness alone. While the framework has clarified why alignment matters, how misalignment develops, and why leadership intent is insufficient to prevent erosion over time, correction requires disciplined construction. Alignment is restored when organizational statements are intentionally built to function as structural instruments that guide behavior and decision-making, rather than as symbolic or aspirational language.

Organizational values, vision, and mission are often treated as expressions of identity or aspiration. When approached this way, they are commonly produced through discussion, consensus, or creative brainstorming. These methods emphasize participation but rarely produce coherence. The result is language that sounds appropriate but lacks the structural integrity to guide behavior, decisions, and priorities consistently.

Effective organizational statements are not written casually. They are constructed deliberately. Construction requires sequence, constraint, and clarity regarding purpose. Each statement must serve a defined role, relate coherently to the others, and operate within a shared framework of meaning. Without this discipline, even well-crafted language can contribute to confusion rather than alignment.

This chapter establishes why disciplined construction is necessary and why the work ahead must be approached as a leadership responsibility rather than a reflective exercise. The goal is not to inspire ideas, but to prepare the reader to engage in a structured process that reduces ambiguity and increases alignment. What follows is not an extension of analysis, but the final preparation for execution.

Failure Is Structural, Not Semantic →

Organizational statements rarely fail because of poor wording. Most organizations can produce language that sounds appropriate, aspirational, and professionally acceptable. Values are phrased positively, visions are future-oriented, and mission statements communicate purpose. Yet misalignment persists, not because the language is unclear, but because the statements themselves lack structural coherence.

When failure is treated as semantic, leaders respond by revising language. Words are adjusted, phrases are softened or sharpened, and new versions are introduced with the expectation that clarity will improve alignment. Over time, this produces cycles of rewriting without resolution. The organization accumulates statements, but behavior, priorities, and decision-making remain inconsistent.

Structural failure occurs when values, vision, and mission are created independently, without defined roles or disciplined sequence. In these conditions, statements may be individually sound but collectively incoherent. Each statement points in a slightly different direction, shaping behavior in competing ways. The issue is not expression, but design.

Because the problem is structural, solutions based on wording alone cannot succeed. Alignment requires that statements function together as an integrated system. This requires intentional construction, clear boundaries, and a shared logic governing how each statement informs the others. Without this structure, language becomes symbolic rather than directive.

Recognizing that failure is structural reframes the task ahead. The work is not to find better words, but to build statements that operate with clarity, coherence, and authority. This distinction is essential before disciplined construction can begin.

Failure Results From Isolation, Not Ignorance →

Organizational misalignment is rarely the result of leaders not knowing what matters. Most leadership teams can clearly articulate what they value, where they want to go, and why the organization exists. The problem is not a lack of understanding, but the way these elements are developed and maintained in isolation from one another.

Values, vision, and mission are often created at different times by different groups for different purposes. Each statement may be reasonable on its own, yet when developed independently, they fail to operate as a unified system. Isolation allows contradictions to persist unnoticed, not because leaders are unaware, but because no disciplined process exists to test coherence across statements.

When isolation becomes normalized, organizations rely on informal alignment. Leaders assume that shared experience, organizational culture, or repeated communication will resolve inconsistencies. In practice, these assumptions increase dependence on interpretation rather than clarity. Employees are left to reconcile competing signals through personal judgment rather than shared structure.

This form of failure is subtle because it does not feel dysfunctional at first. Statements exist, conversations occur, and intentions remain sincere. Over time, however, isolation produces fragmentation. Decisions become situational, priorities shift without explanation, and accountability weakens. The organization functions, but without directional consistency.

Addressing this failure requires integration, not education. The corrective task is not to teach leaders what values, vision, or mission are, but to construct them in relation to one another. Disciplined alignment replaces isolated development, ensuring that each statement reinforces rather than competes with the others.

Failure Persists Even In Sincere Organizations →

Organizational misalignment often persists not because leaders lack integrity or commitment, but because sincerity alone cannot correct structural weaknesses. Many organizations operate with genuine concern for their people, clear moral intent, and a strong desire to do what is right. These qualities, while important, do not substitute for disciplined design.

Sincere organizations often assume that shared values or goodwill will naturally lead to alignment. When problems emerge, they respond by reaffirming intent, increasing communication, or emphasizing culture. These responses feel appropriate because they are consistent with the organization's character. However, they do not address the structural conditions that allow misalignment to continue.

The persistence of failure in sincere organizations is particularly difficult to recognize because effort is visible and ongoing. Leaders meet, statements are discussed, and language is reaffirmed. The organization appears active and engaged, yet direction remains unclear. In these situations, activity replaces alignment, and motion is mistaken for progress.

Sincerity can unintentionally mask structural deficiencies. When leaders care deeply, they are less likely to question whether the underlying design of their organizational statements is contributing to confusion. This creates resistance to disciplined reconstruction, not out of arrogance, but out of trust in good intentions.

Recognizing that sincerity does not prevent failure is a necessary step toward correction. Alignment requires more than commitment. It requires structures that translate intent into clarity and coherence. Until those structures are intentionally built, misalignment can persist even in the healthiest and most well-meaning organizations.

Alignment Is Not Intuitive →

Organizational alignment is often assumed to emerge naturally when capable leaders work together in good faith. Shared experience, frequent communication, and mutual respect are expected to produce clarity over time. In practice, these conditions do not reliably create alignment. They create familiarity, not structure.

Intuition is shaped by experience, but experience is fragmented across roles, responsibilities, and perspectives. Leaders interpret organizational priorities through the lens of their own functions, pressures, and incentives. Without a disciplined structure, these interpretations remain personal rather than shared, even when underlying intentions are aligned.

Alignment requires more than agreement on broad ideas. It requires clarity about sequence, boundaries, and function. Values, vision, and mission must each serve a distinct role and operate in a defined relationship to one another. These relationships are not self-evident. When they are left implicit, leaders fill the gaps with assumptions, and assumptions produce inconsistency.

The belief that alignment is intuitive encourages informal processes. Statements are developed through discussion, compromise, or creative brainstorming, with the expectation that coherence will emerge through conversation. These methods privilege participation but rarely produce precision. Over time, they increase ambiguity rather than reduce it.

Recognizing that alignment is not intuitive reframes leadership's responsibility. The task is not to feel aligned, but to build alignment. This requires discipline, structure, and intentional constraint. Without these elements, even experienced leaders will continue to rely on intuition where construction is required.

Leaders Assume Alignment Happens Naturally →

Leadership teams often assume that alignment will develop as relationships mature and experience accumulates. Time spent working together, shared challenges, and repeated interaction are expected to produce a common understanding of priorities and direction. While these factors increase familiarity, they do not produce structural alignment.

This assumption is reinforced by visible cooperation. Meetings function smoothly, language appears consistent, and disagreements are resolved collegially. These signals create confidence that alignment exists, even when underlying interpretations of values, vision, and mission differ significantly. The absence of conflict is mistaken for coherence.

Natural alignment is further assumed when organizations rely heavily on culture. Culture can reinforce shared behavior, but it cannot correct unclear structure. When statements lack defined roles or relationships, culture compensates through habit and precedent. This allows organizations to function, but it does not ensure directional clarity or consistency over time.

The belief that alignment happens naturally reduces the perceived need for disciplined construction. Leaders postpone structural work because operations continue and results appear acceptable. Over time, however, untested assumptions accumulate. Decisions become situational, priorities shift subtly, and accountability weakens without a clear point of reference.

Recognizing this assumption is critical. Alignment does not emerge through proximity, experience, or goodwill. It must be intentionally constructed. Without disciplined design, organizations rely on appearance rather than structure, and misalignment remains undetected until it becomes costly.

Alignment Requires Constraint, Order, And Definition ⟶

Alignment does not emerge from openness alone. It requires constraint. Constraints limit interpretation, reduce ambiguity, and establish boundaries within which decisions are made. Without constraint, organizational statements invite personal meaning rather than shared direction. Clarity is replaced by flexibility, and flexibility becomes inconsistency.

Order is equally necessary. Values, vision, and mission cannot be developed simultaneously or interchangeably without undermining their function. Each statement serves a distinct role and must be constructed in a deliberate sequence. When order is ignored, statements compete rather than reinforce one another. The result is language that appears comprehensive but lacks internal logic.

The definition completes the structure. Terms such as purpose, direction, priorities, and values must be explicitly defined within the organization's context. Undefined language relies on assumptions, and assumptions vary across roles and levels. When a definition is absent, alignment becomes dependent on interpretation rather than structure.

Constraints, orders, and definitions are often resisted because they feel limiting. In reality, they are enabling. They reduce the need for clarification, debate, and reinterpretation. They allow organizational statements to function as reference points rather than discussion starters.

Alignment is not the product of shared intention. It is the result of disciplined design. Constraint, order, and definition provide the conditions under which alignment can be sustained rather than assumed.

Creativity Without Structure Increases Misalignment →

Creativity is often treated as a prerequisite for developing organizational statements. Leaders are encouraged to generate ideas freely, explore language collaboratively, and allow meaning to emerge through discussion. While creativity has a role, it cannot substitute for structure. When creativity is unconstrained, it amplifies divergence rather than alignment.

In unstructured settings, participants contribute ideas shaped by personal experience, functional priorities, and individual interpretation. The result is a wide range of inputs that feel rich but lack coherence. Language becomes inclusive rather than precise, accommodating multiple meanings instead of establishing shared direction. What feels collaborative in the moment produces ambiguity over time.

Creative processes also tend to reward originality rather than clarity. Phrases that sound compelling or distinctive are favored, even when their functional role is unclear. Over time, statements become symbolic artifacts rather than operational references. Employees learn to appreciate the language without relying on it to guide decisions.

Without structure, creativity shifts the burden of alignment onto interpretation. Leaders and employees must continually reconcile meaning through conversation, explanation, and adjustment. This creates dependency on leadership presence rather than organizational design. Alignment becomes fragile, maintained through effort rather than reinforced through structure.

Creativity is most effective when it operates within defined constraints. Structure channels creativity toward clarity rather than expansion. When constraint, order, and definition are established first, creativity refines meaning instead of multiplying interpretations. Without that structure, creativity does not solve misalignment; it accelerates it.

Statement Creation as a Leadership Act →

Organizational statements are not neutral artifacts. They establish direction, define priorities, and shape how decisions are justified over time. Because of this, their creation carries authority, whether or not that authority is acknowledged. When statements exist, they influence behavior. The only question is whether that influence is coherent or fragmented.

In many organizations, statement creation is treated as an administrative task rather than a leadership responsibility. Language is developed through committees, creative sessions, or iterative revisions designed to preserve participation and consensus. These processes distribute involvement but dilute ownership. When no one is accountable for coherence, alignment becomes incidental rather than intentional.

Leadership in statement creation does not require unilateral authorship, but it does require responsibility for structure. Leaders must ensure that values, vision, and mission are deliberately constructed in sequence and in relationship to one another. This responsibility cannot be delegated to culture, collaboration, or external facilitation without introducing fragmentation. Authority that is diffused cannot enforce coherence.

Statement creation also forces leaders to confront constraints. Decisions must be made about what the organization will prioritize, what it will exclude, and how success will be defined. These decisions involve trade-offs that cannot be resolved through inclusive language. Avoiding trade-offs produces statements that are broad, agreeable, and operationally weak. Leadership is expressed not through comprehensiveness but through clarity.

When leaders treat statement creation as a leadership act, the work's purpose shifts. The objective is no longer inspiration or alignment through agreement. The objective becomes disciplined construction that translates intent into structure. This reframing is necessary before any structured process can succeed.

Statements Are Instruments, Not Expressions ⟶

Organizational statements function as instruments. They are designed to shape behavior, guide decisions, and establish boundaries over time. Their purpose is operational, not expressive. When statements are treated as expressions of identity, belief, or aspiration, their ability to produce alignment is weakened.

Expressions invite interpretation. Instruments impose reference. An expressive statement allows individuals to locate their own meaning within the language. An instrumental statement limits meaning to create consistency. This distinction is often overlooked because expressive language feels authentic and inclusive. Over time, however, inclusion without constraints leads to fragmentation.

When statements are designed as instruments, their effectiveness is measured by how they are used rather than how they are received. They must be capable of informing decisions, resolving ambiguity, and justifying priorities without continual explanation. Language that requires interpretation or reinforcement fails to perform this function reliably.

Treating statements as instruments also requires intentional design. Instruments are built for specific purposes, tested under expected use conditions, and refined to reduce variability. Organizational statements require the same discipline. Their structure, scope, and relationship to one another must be defined in advance, not discovered through use.

Reframing statements as instruments clarifies the work ahead. The task is not to express what the organization believes, but to construct reference points that govern how the organization operates. This shift is necessary before disciplined statement construction can begin.

Decisions Must Precede Language →

Organizational language cannot resolve uncertainty that leadership has not yet confronted. Words are incapable of carrying decisions that have not been made. When statements are written before decisions are clarified, language becomes a substitute for leadership rather than an expression of it. The result is wording that sounds deliberate while masking unresolved direction.

Many organizations reverse the proper sequence. They begin with language in order to discover agreement, hoping that discussion will reveal priorities. In practice, this approach transfers decision-making into phrasing. Choices about direction, emphasis, and limitation are deferred into word selection rather than addressed directly. Language becomes negotiable because the decisions behind it remain unsettled.

Decisions precede language because alignment requires resolution before expression. Leaders must determine what the organization will prioritize, what it will subordinate, and what it will intentionally exclude. These determinations are structural, not semantic. They exist independently of how they are eventually articulated. Until these decisions are made, language remains provisional and unstable.

When language is developed prematurely, it absorbs unresolved tension. Statements attempt to accommodate competing priorities rather than order them. Broad phrasing replaces clarity. Ambiguity is preserved to avoid conflict. While this may reduce immediate resistance, it embeds contradiction into the organization's foundational references. Over time, those contradictions surface in inconsistent decisions, shifting priorities, and unclear accountability.

Preceding language with decision-making also clarifies ownership. Decisions require authority. Language can be edited collaboratively, but decisions cannot be crowdsourced without losing coherence. When leaders avoid decision-making by moving directly to language, they distribute responsibility without distributing clarity. The organization receives words, but not direction.

Disciplined statement construction requires leaders to separate the decision from expression. Decisions establish the structure. Language gives that structure form. Reversing this sequence undermines both. Language cannot compensate for indecision, nor can it resolve tensions leaders are unwilling to address.

Placing decisions before language changes the nature of the work ahead. The task is no longer to find the right words, but to make the right determinations. Once those determinations are clear, language becomes precise rather than symbolic. Alignment becomes possible because structure exists before expression.

Trade-Offs Are Unavoidable And Necessary →

Alignment requires exclusion. Every organizational statement implies a preference, and preferences require trade-offs.

Attempting to avoid trade-offs does not preserve unity; it obscures direction. When leaders refuse to choose, language is forced to carry incompatible priorities, and misalignment is embedded at the structural level.

Many organizations resist trade-offs because they appear divisive or restrictive. Leaders fear that choosing one emphasis over another will alienate stakeholders, limit flexibility, or close future options. As a result, statements are written to include as much as possible. Breadth is mistaken for strength. In practice, inclusivity without prioritization weakens authority and creates uncertainty about what truly matters.

Trade-offs clarify intent. They signal what the organization will protect, pursue, and prioritize when resources are constrained or pressures compete. Without trade-offs, statements cannot guide decisions because they do not resolve tension. When everything is important, nothing governs. Decision-making becomes situational, and alignment depends on context rather than structure.

Avoiding trade-offs also shifts the burden of interpretation downward. When statements lack clear prioritization, employees are forced to infer what takes precedence. This produces inconsistency across departments, leaders, and situations. The organization appears aligned in principle but fragmented in practice. Over time, this erodes accountability because expectations were never clearly established.

Trade-offs are not signs of rigidity. They are signs of leadership. They reflect an organization's willingness to accept limitations in service of clarity. Well-constructed statements do not attempt to represent every value, aspiration, or possibility. They represent what will govern decisions when competing pressures arise.

Accepting trade-offs is essential to disciplined construction. Values must be ranked rather than listed. Vision must focus on direction rather than describe every future. Mission must define purpose rather than justify all activity. These distinctions cannot be achieved through language alone. They require prior determination and deliberate exclusion.

Trade-offs are unavoidable because alignment demands structure. They are necessary because structure enables coherence. Until leaders accept this reality, statement creation will remain aspirational rather than directive, and misalignment will persist regardless of intent.

Readiness for Disciplined Construction →

The purpose of this chapter has not been to introduce additional concepts, but to establish readiness. Organizational alignment cannot be achieved through awareness, intention, or expression alone. It requires disciplined construction grounded in clear decisions, accepted trade-offs, and defined structure. Without these elements, statement creation reproduces the same conditions that allow misalignment to persist.

Readiness is not measured by confidence or enthusiasm. It is measured by constraint. Leaders are ready to proceed when they understand that values, vision, and mission must be built in sequence, with defined roles and explicit relationships. Readiness exists when language is no longer treated as discovery, but as articulation of decisions already made.

The work ahead requires restraint. The process will limit options, reduce ambiguity, and force prioritization. This is intentional. Disciplined construction does not attempt to capture every idea or preserve every preference. It establishes reference points that govern behavior, guide decisions, and sustain alignment over time. Entering this process without accepting its constraints undermines its purpose.

The Values, Vision, and Mission workbooks that follow are designed to impose this discipline. They do not function as reflective exercises or creative prompts. They exist to control variables, enforce sequence, and reduce interpretive misalignment. Their structure is not incidental. It is essential.

This chapter concludes the framework phase of the work. What follows is construction. The reader now possesses the language, logic, and posture required to engage that work responsibly. The task ahead is not to explore what alignment could be, but to build the structures that make alignment possible.

The Framework Has Established Shared Language ⟶

The framework has established a shared language necessary for disciplined construction. Terms such as alignment, misalignment, values, vision, mission, structure, and coherence have been defined intentionally rather than assumed. This shared language is not cosmetic. It provides the foundation required to reduce interpretation and ensure that subsequent work proceeds from a common understanding rather than individual inference.

Without shared language, creating organizational statements becomes an exercise in translation. Participants use the same words while assigning different meanings, creating the appearance of agreement without actual alignment. The framework phase has addressed this risk by clarifying how key terms function within an integrated system rather than as isolated concepts.

Shared language also establishes boundaries. It limits how terms may be used and prevents them from being stretched to accommodate competing priorities. This constraint is essential. Disciplined construction depends on precision, and precision cannot exist where language remains flexible or undefined.

By completing the framework, the reader no longer approaches statement creation as a conceptual discussion. The language required for construction is now fixed, consistent, and operational. This does not eliminate disagreement, but it ensures that disagreement occurs within a shared structure rather than across competing definitions.

The establishment of shared language marks a critical threshold. It signals that the work ahead is no longer interpretive. It is constructive. With language clarified, the remaining task is to apply it through a disciplined process rather than continued explanation.

You Are Now Accountable For Coherence →

With shared language established, responsibility shifts. Coherence cannot be attributed to misunderstanding, terminology, or conceptual ambiguity. The framework has provided the definitions, distinctions, and logic required for alignment. What remains is the responsibility to apply them consistently.

Accountability for coherence means that values, vision, and mission must no longer be evaluated independently. Each statement must be tested against the others for compatibility, reinforcement, and internal consistency. Incoherence is no longer a theoretical risk; it becomes a leadership failure when tolerated or ignored.

This accountability also changes how statements are judged. Language is no longer sufficient on its own. Statements must demonstrate functional alignment. They must point in the same direction, support the same priorities, and justify the same decisions. Where tension exists, it must be resolved structurally rather than explained away rhetorically.

The reader's role at this stage is not interpretive. It is integrative. Decisions made in one statement must be honored in the others. Definitions must remain stable. Priorities must remain visible. Allowing misalignment at this stage reintroduces the very conditions the framework has identified as harmful.

Accountability for coherence is not shared broadly or deferred indefinitely. It resides with leadership. The framework has completed its work by clarifying what coherence requires. The next phase tests whether that clarity will be enforced through disciplined construction or compromised through convenience.

The Work Ahead Is Sequential And Intentional →

The work that follows is not open-ended. It proceeds in sequence and with intent. Values, vision, and mission are not interchangeable components, nor can they be constructed simultaneously without undermining coherence. Each statement builds upon the clarity established by the one before it. Sequence is not a preference; it is a structural requirement.

Intentionality governs this sequence. Each step limits the next by design. Decisions made in the values stage constrain vision. Vision clarifies the direction that the mission must serve. This progression prevents contradiction and reduces interpretive misalignment. Skipping steps or reversing the order weakens the system's integrity and reintroduces ambiguity.

Sequential work also resists urgency. Disciplined construction cannot be rushed without sacrificing clarity. The temptation to move quickly, finalize language, or resolve discomfort prematurely undermines the purpose of the process. Intentional pacing ensures that decisions are made before language and that trade-offs are addressed rather than deferred.

This structure may feel restrictive, particularly for leaders accustomed to flexibility and adaptive language. In practice, it is stabilizing. A sequence reduces rework, prevents cyclical revisions, and establishes durable reference points. Alignment becomes sustainable when it is deliberately built rather than negotiated continuously.

The work ahead requires adherence to process. The discipline is not optional, and the order is not arbitrary. These constraints exist to protect coherence. With the framework complete, the next step is disciplined construction through the LCSM10 Values workbook, the LCSM10 Vision workbook, and the LCSM10 Mission workbook. These workbooks provide the structured process necessary to translate decisions into coherent organizational statements and to sustain alignment over time.

Final Commissioning: From Architecture to Execution

This work has established the leadership architecture of the Lucas Customer Satisfaction Model 10. You now possess the governing framework required to build aligned organizational systems with discipline, coherence, and accountability. You have examined the cost of misalignment. You have studied the structure of leadership clarity. You have seen that alignment is not intuitive. You have learned that organizational health is not accidental.

This framework governs how leaders think, decide, build, and lead. It establishes the authority structure of leadership. It defines how belief becomes behavior, how direction becomes execution, and how purpose is protected through governance. You are now accountable for coherence. The work ahead is no longer conceptual. It is constructive.

Alignment is not created through inspiration. It is built through disciplined leadership decisions, structured design, and enforced standards. Statements are not expressions. They are instruments. Values, vision, and mission must now be constructed with precision, tested for alignment, and protected through leadership systems. This book governs. The LCSM10 Implementation Series executes. Leadership stewards both.

The next phase of the LCSM10 system is disciplined statement construction through the LCSM10 Implementation Series. These workbooks provide the structured frameworks, scoring logic, construction models, and alignment disciplines required to translate leadership decisions into coherent organizational statements and to sustain alignment over time.

The LCSM10 Implementation Series includes the LCSM10 Values Workbook, the LCSM10 Vision Workbook, and the LCSM10 Mission Workbook.

These workbooks are not a curriculum. They are leadership instruments. They are designed for senior leadership, boards, founders, and executive teams who carry responsibility for organizational direction, culture, strategy, and governance.

The LCSM10 Consulting Toolkit is designed for consultants seeking disciplined engagement structure, defensible diagnostics, repeatable scoring, governance-aligned reconstruction, and certification-level alignment verification. It provides the architectural foundation that supports, governs, and protects the statement construction process.

Organizational statements should not be constructed without disciplined structure. The effectiveness of the LCSM10 system depends on sequence, order, and constraint. Architecture must precede construction. Authority must precede execution. Decisions must precede language.

The framework is now complete. The language is now established. The responsibility now rests with you. The work ahead is intentional. The work ahead is disciplined. The work ahead is consequential. This is where alignment is built.

www.ingramcontent.com/pod-product-compliance
Lightning Source LLC
LaVergne TN
LVHW010607110826
845149LV00003B/811